I0416515

Bold Business Wealth:The Art of Building Business Fortunes Without Fear and Strategies of Smart Entrepreneurship

By

Jose R. Johnson

Copyright ©,2024

Table of contents:

INTRODUCTION

The allure of reaching overflow without taking a chance is a constant delusion in the rainbow of audacious aspirations, seductive but unstable. Every self-assured industry tycoon's journey always starts with a well-known desire to hoard abundance without venturing into the misleading waters of possibility. It's a thought murmured in meeting rooms and bistros, where self-assured visionaries of business scribble their fantasies on napkins, and in the lobbies of new organizations. Regardless, the notion of chance-free wealth is essentially as false as a desert garden that offers salvation but reveals nothing more than shifting sands.

Deciphering the Twofold Transaction

Prior to embarking on the mission of business overflow without risk, we should remove the layers of deceit that envelop the leading scene. It's a trip to the heart of adventurous No win scenarios are those in which risk and reward engage in an unending tango, with every step carrying a heavy weight of possibility for success or failure. Investigating the double dealing necessitates a serious analysis of the dreams that routinely obscure the overflow creation reality.

We will refute the myth that success can be attained without encountering the arbitrary expansions of possibility in this unfolding narrative. The wounds received in the fight against weakness are hidden behind the tall tales of successful business magnates. Through their experiences, we discover that the wager is an ill-defined mate who is trying to survive rather than the enemy.

The Illustration of Wealth in Business

It becomes evident as we delve deeper into the source of business wealth that conquering risk is more important than mitigating it. The core of business overflow is a web of advancement, flexibility, and essential information. It's an adventure where chance transforms from an incredible enemy to a notable ally, providing unobstructed pathways to growth, education, and unmatched success.

Understanding the elements of a constantly developing business focus is essential to comprehending the essence of business overflow. It is an acknowledgement that the pursuit of fortune is a formidable endeavor that calls for flexibility and a keen understanding of the relationship between risk and reward. We dive right into the tales of associations that have weathered storms by seizing opportunity rather than running from it and using it to drive unparalleled success.

In the upcoming sections, we will examine the components of business overflow that go beyond the boundaries of the tested viewpoint. Our interaction serves as a compass to coordinate money managers through the peculiar spaces of overflow creation, covering everything from the fundamentals of developing a solid business foundation to the subtleties of wise assumptions and creative strategies.

As we stand on the precipice of this test, poised between objective and validation, let us banish the myth of luck-free wealth and welcome the real, amazing influence of audacious effort. In the pages that follow, we will dissect the intricacies, demystify the obstacles, and plot a path that, in light of the cornerstone of fearless business, leads not just to wealth but also to a legacy.

The odyssey commences, with the objective being the ultimate measure of success.

CHAPTER 1:

The Establishment: Building a Strong Business Base

Encouraging areas of strength for a foundation is like laying the reason for a solid development - one that gets through regular difficulty and supports the weight of desires. In this examination of "The Foundation: Building Areas of strength for a Base," we will jump into the key guidelines that help a prospering endeavor. From picking the right game plan to procedures for reasonable turn of events, our interaction begins at the groundwork of inventive accomplishment.

Picking the Right Game plan

The graph of a productive business is erratically joined to the decision of a legitimate strategy. In the immense scene of spearheading likely results, each model conveys its own course of action of advantages, risks, and components. Confident business people habitually end up at the convergence, taking into account whether to embrace a traditional model, plunge into online business, or examine the problematic space of tech new organizations.

Figuring out Game plans

To seek after informed decisions, money managers ought to understand the intricacies of various game plans. From the dependable foundation model to the participation based approach, each model lines up with unquestionable market components and solicitations a custom fitted technique for progress. The outing begins with an examination of these models, dismantling their nuances and surveying their likeness with the envisioned undertaking.

Fitting the Model to Your Vision

The one-size-fits-all approach isn't invite there of psyche of strategies. A successful finance manager is one who appreciates the intricacies of each model as well as creators it to suit the clever vision and potential gains of the endeavor.

We plunge into relevant examinations of associations that have flourished by changing and propelling inside their picked model, revealing the historic power of essential plan.

Techniques for Viable Turn of events

With the game plan as the compass, useful improvement transforms into the North Star coordinating the finance manager's journey. Improvement is certainly not a goal yet a tireless turn of events, mentioning a fundamental procedure that transcends transitory increments. The supporting of areas of strength for a base lays on the execution of improvement strategies that develop life range and flexibility.

Building a Flexible Structure

Conservative improvement requires a generous establishment that can conform to the changing solicitations of the market. From flexible advancement deals with deft definitive plans, we research the construction blocks of an establishment that maintains flow errands as well as expects and obliges future turns of events.

Investigating Business area Components

The ambitious outing is a significant part of the time depicted by fluctuating business area components. Understanding and investigating these components are premier to upheld accomplishment. We break down the methods used by viable associations in acclimating to publicize shifts, embracing headway, and rapidly making the most of chances amidst challenges.

Fostering a Client Driven Approach

At the center of legitimate improvement lies a huge commitment to the client. Associations that overcome are those that attention on customer unwaveringness, responsibility, and immovability. We unravel the procedures used by industry trailblazers to foster a client driven culture, making trades as well as getting through associations.

Context oriented examinations in Foundation Building

To improve how we could decipher building serious areas of strength for a base, we leave on an outing through the narratives of business history. Logical examinations from various organizations show off the usage of these focal guidelines. From the ascending of tech beasts to the adaptability of family-guaranteed tries, each story contributes critical guides to our examination.

The Framework of Achievement

The Mind study of Route

The foundation of a solid business base connects past the essential parts; it plunges into the psychological spaces of route. Business visionaries are engineers as well as clinicians, understanding the intricacies of client direct, market designs, and the art of impact.

Client Cerebrum research: Unraveling Needs

A significant cognizance of client mind research empowers business visionaries to design things and organizations that resonate with the desires and prerequisites of their ideal vested party. We examine the principles of client lead, the effect of sentiments on free course, and the mind exploration of denoting that designs persevering through affiliations.

Key Free course: Investigating Weakness

The business scene is spilling over with weaknesses, and key free course is the compass that guides business visionaries through the fog. From risk assessment to opportunity affirmation, we plunge into the psychological cycles that help effective bearing, furnishing business visionaries with the mental instruments to investigate the complexities of business.

Advancement and Adaptability

The underpinning of areas of strength for a foundation is improvement. It isn't just a famous articulation anyway a mindset that immerses each piece of the endeavor. We explore the remarkable power of progression, from thing improvement to useful efficiency, and inspect how associations can foster a culture of diligent improvement.

Embracing Creative Movements

In the mechanized age, mechanical improvement is a primary driving force behind business accomplishment. We dive into logical examinations of associations that have outfitted the power of advancement to streamline exercises, contact greater groups, and stay ahead in merciless business areas.

The Agile Financial specialist: Thriving in Change

Adaptability is a capacity to get by in the novel scene of business. We break down the characteristics of composed business visionaries who embrace change as well as prosper in it. From turning strategies to rebranding methodology, we loosen up the stories of associations that have changed hardships into open entryways through flexibility.

Building a Brand That Drives forward

The brand is more than a logo or a trademark; it is the soul of the business. Building a brand that overcomes requires a fundamental strategy that goes past exhibiting endeavors. We break down the parts of successful stamping, from describing to validity, and explore how associations can cut an undeniable character watching out.

Describing: Partner with Groups

In a period overpowered by information over-trouble, describing transforms into an astonishing resource for associations to communicate with their group on a more significant level. We explore the specialty of describing in checking, showing how associations can twist around stories that resonate with their characteristics and attract clients deep down.

Validness: The Bedrock of Trust

In our ongoing reality where believability is an exceptional thing, associations that overflow legitimacy manufacture depend with their group. We analyze the meaning of realness in checking, taking a gander at how associations can change their characteristics to their illuminating to make a brand that perseveres for a very extensive stretch.

Supporting Accomplishment: The Occupation of Organization
Responsible for every single productive business is a visionary boss. We examine the characteristics of convincing drive, from developing a positive various leveled culture to making fundamental decisions that push the business ahead.

Authority Styles: Changing in accordance with Hardships
Convincing drive is certainly not a one-size-fits-all proposal. Different hardships demand different power styles. We separate different organization styles, from historic to situational drive, and inspect how trailblazers can change their ways of managing address the

wonderful solicitations of their business environment.

Various leveled Culture: Supporting Accomplishment

The lifestyle of an affiliation is the indistinct power that shapes its destiny. We plunge into the meaning of progressive culture in supporting accomplishment, researching how associations can develop a positive, helpful, and creative culture that attracts top capacity and holds laborers.

The Occupation of Ethics and Social Commitment

The foundation of a solid business base connects past advantages to incorporate ethics and social commitment. We examine the occupation of associations in contributing positively to society, watching out for regular concerns, and partaking in moral practices that resonate with current clients.

Corporate Social Commitment: Past Advantage

In a period where customers are dynamically mindful of the social and environmental impact of their choices, corporate social commitment (CSR) isn't just a choice yet an objective. We discuss the guidelines of CSR, showing associations that have really integrated social and regular crashes into their middle undertakings.

Moral Heading: Investigating Cloudy circumstances

Moral route is a compass that guides associations through the complexities of current exchange. We take a gander at relevant examinations of associations that have faced moral circumstances and research the procedures used to investigate the badly characterized circumstances, keeping up with guidelines while ensuring sensibility.

Investigating the Financial Scene

Getting a handle on Adventure Significant entryways

The financial scene is a scene weighed down with important entryways and risks. Money managers ought to investigate this scene with insight and feeling, making fundamental hypothesis decisions that fuel improvement and reduce anticipated disasters.

Adventure Basics: A Primer

For financial specialists meandering into the money related area, sorting out the basics of speculations is indispensable. We research the stray pieces of adventure, from stocks and bonds to land, giving a thorough fundamental to business people attempting to make informed financial decisions.

Risk The board in Hypotheses

Contributing is inherently appended to risk, yet it isn't indivisible from silliness. We dive into the norms of chance organization in adventures, discussing strategies for assessing, directing, and using peril to smooth out returns.

Financial Expecting Long stretch Accomplishment

A solid financial foundation requires cautious readiness. From intending to guaging, we unravel the basic pieces of financial orchestrating that add to the excessively long advancement of associations.

Arranging: A Diagram for Money related Prosperity

Arranging isn't just a money related gadget; it is a layout for the financial prosperity of the business. We discuss the norms of convincing preparation, examining how associations can allocate resources conclusively to intensify efficiency and advantage.

Financial Assessing: Anticipating What the future holds

The ability to expect money related designs is a mastery that isolates compelling associations. We explore the art of money related assessing, analyzing how associations can use irrefutable data, market assessment, and industry examples to make informed figures about their financial future.

Going with Informed Money related Decisions

Money related decisions are the foundation of a business, shaping its bearing and influencing its solidarity even with monetary challenges. We examine the powerful cycles drew in with financial organization, from capital wanting to subsidizing decisions.

Capital Preparation: Distributing Resources Definitively

Effective capital arranging is the underpinning of resource assignment. We analyze the principles of capital preparation, showing how associations can conclusively appropriate resources for projects that make the main yields.

Subsidizing Philosophies: Past the Fundamental concern

The choice of financing approaches has critical consequences for the money related adequacy of the business. We research different financing decisions, from commitment supporting to esteem subsidizing, discussing the components that money managers should consider while chasing after subsidizing decisions.

Logical examinations in Money related Predominance

To edify the principles of investigating the financial scene, we dive into logical examinations of associations that have become astounding at money related organization. From minimal new organizations to worldwide endeavors, each context oriented investigation offers significant pieces of information into the frameworks used to gain financial headway.

Publicizing Expert for Business Accomplishment

Fruitful Checking and Arranging

Stuck pressed business place, strong checking and arranging are not just frameworks; they are objectives. We examine the parts of productive checking, from making a persuading brand character to definitively arranging the business in the characters of buyers.

Making a Persuading Brand Character

The brand character is the embodiment of the business, conveying its characteristics, character, and responsibilities. We inspect the parts of a persuading brand character, examining how associations can make a brand that reverberates with their fundamental vested party.

Indispensable Arranging: Enthralling everybody

Arranging is the specialty of partition, and in a ferocious scene, standing separated is indistinguishable from progress. We dive into the norms of key arranging, inspecting how associations can cut a specific specialty watching out and turn into the leaned toward choice for their clients.

Interacting with Your Vested party

Promoting isn't just about things; it's about people. We explore the methodology for connecting with the vested party on a more significant level, from sorting out buyer direct to using the power of up close and personal advancing.

Purchaser Direct: Interpreting the Market

A significant cognizance of customer direct is the best approach to convincing exhibiting. We discuss the guidelines of client lead, examining how associations can unwind the market, anticipate necessities, and originator their promoting frameworks to resonate with their group.

Significant Promoting: Forming Persevering through Affiliations

In a period overpowered by modernized upheaval, significant exhibiting is an aide that cuts through the untidiness. We explore the specialty of significant publicizing, showing associations that have really formed getting through relationship with their group by addressing sentiments and values.

Using Progressed Advancing Procedures

The high level scene has reshaped the advancing perspective, offering unprecedented entryways for associations to contact greater groups. We explore the norms of cutting edge exhibiting, from content creation to online amusement methods, giving encounters into how associations can harness the power of the modernized area.

Content Publicizing: The Art of Describing

Content exhibiting is more than an example; it is a significant change in how associations talk with their group. We discuss the guidelines of content exhibiting, exploring how associations can utilize the art of describing to interface with, instruct, and propel their group.

Online Theater setups: Past Inclinations and Offers

Electronic diversion isn't just a phase for inclinations and offers; it is a strong space where associations can connect with their group persistently. We research reasonable virtual diversion strategies, inspecting how associations can create solid areas for a presence and foster a neighborhood unflinching enthusiasts.

Context oriented examinations in Displaying Authority

To exemplify the guidelines of advancing predominance, we dive into relevant examinations of associations that have had an enormous impact through their displaying procedures. From guerrilla publicizing endeavors to viral sensations, each context oriented examination offers critical outlines for associations hoping to lift their displaying game.

Genuine Shields: Protecting Your Wealth

Real Fundamentals for Business visionaries

Pursuing flood, authentic securities are not just wellbeing endeavors; they are necessities. We take a gander at the genuine basics that business visionaries ought to consider, from picking the right business improvement to understanding protected movement regards.

Picking the Right Business Progression

The choice of business structure has essential implications for veritable obligation, charge assessment, and useful adaptability. We analyze the different business structures, from sole proprietorships to affiliations, giving encounters into how finance managers can get the improvement that lines with their goals and safeguards their inclinations.

Safeguarded progress Commendations: Protecting New turn of events

In a period where improvement is an essential position, protecting supported development is chief. We take a gander at the principles of endorsed movement astonishing entryways, inspecting how affiliations can protect their turns of events, picture names, and inventive works.

Inspecting Approaches and Plans

The way that ties business affiliations goes with procedures and outlines the black magic. We bounce into the intricacies of understanding standard, looking at the bits of a liberal strategy and giving encounters into how affiliations can investigate really keeping relationship with moderate risks and affirmation consistence.

Drafting Strong Blueprints

Strong cognizance drafting is a workmanship that requires exactness and hunch. We look at the bits of a particularly made understanding, examining how affiliations can draft plans that sort out hypotheses, convey bets, and give a guaranteed framework to the relationship.

Contract Trade and Question Objective

Trade is a skill that points of interaction past the social event room; it is a gigantic piece of settling discussions and staying aware of sound business affiliations. We research the norms of understanding trade, looking at procedures for achieving normally significant outcomes and settling conflicts with the ultimate objective that jam business affiliations.

As we close this examination of building areas of strength for a base, obviously the foundation is more than an essential part — a straightforward substance creates with the remarkable thought of business. The creative trip is a ceaseless mission to empower and broaden this foundation, to manufacture a legacy that transcends ages.

We will examine the complexities of hazard the board, development, showcasing dominance, and legitimate shields in the accompanying sections — each adding to an organization's flexibility and success. Our establishment is rarely static; it's a material whereupon we paint the story of our spearheading odyssey. The request isn't simply the manner by which well we lay the primary blocks yet how capably we investigate the challenges and entryways that arise as the development rises.

The journey continues, and the foundation is by the by the beginning.

CHAPTER 2:

Chance Administration Demystified

The gamble the board interaction is a fundamental piece of the general way your association answers risk. Furthermore, when the business climate feels intrinsically unsafe - like in the midst of financial choppiness, progress or disturbance - it merits requiring a little investment to survey your gamble the board approach.

Your gamble the board system is the administration structure that executes and upholds the interaction. So how about we single out the gamble interaction for now, and survey how that ought to function.

1. RISK Recognizable proof
The most vital phase in the gamble the board cycle is generally to recognize what dangers are out there. Dangers can be potential open doors

(positive things that are questionable) or risks (negative things that are unsure), connected with consistence or control, or whatever other arrangement that sounds good to your business.

Risk distinguishing proof is certainly not an oddball work out. It's something individuals contemplate in the midst of disturbance, however it ought to be a continuous exertion for your groups. The most straightforward method for doing this is to plan time for it. Whether that is essential for the PMO's liability, or whether it sits with the gamble administration group - for however long somebody is routinely auditing the exercises and undertakings in the business and recognizing new dangers, then, at that point, you're brilliant.

2. RISK Investigation

Risk investigation is the following stage. Whenever you have recognized what dangers are confronting the association, division, group or task, you ought to break down the circumstance to ensure it is completely perceived.

Frequently, investigation hurls a few fascinating elements that probably won't have been as expected considered until this point. Acquire your well-informed authorities and plunge into what has been going on with lead you to this present circumstance. Consider who else should be involved. What could the following stages be?

Examination and assessment frequently occur in equal and are interpreted as meaning comparative things. As a component of your examination, work out the effect should the gamble occur. The effect can be estimated in monetary, quality, time or whatever other measure that squeezes into your classification framework.

At long last, take a gander at the probability that the gamble will occur. A few dangers are undeniably bound to happen than others. These are the ones you need to focus on in the subsequent stage, so you have your arrangements immovably ready before the gamble occurs. Furthermore, in the event that it doesn't, indeed, it's smarter to be ready!

3. RISK TREATMENT

Whenever you have finished the gamble investigation step, the group sorts out what choices are available to them to deal with the gamble. This is regularly finished by having the specialists in the room (or meeting practically) and conceptualizing the various ways the gamble could be drawn nearer. They'll then concoct a proposal for subsequent stages.

The gamble treatment is drawn from various choices. For instance:

- Alleviation (Decrease)
- Acknowledgment (Disregard)
- Transaction
- Evasion
- Share

You might utilize a mix of techniques, or a few in progression, to deal with the gamble as per the test it presents for your business or undertaking.

Keep in mind, with positive/opportunity risk, you'll believe your administration activities should attempt to make the gamble as logical as conceivable to happen. How might you steer the results and make it more probable that you'll end up in that? Then how might you benefit from it? This is the 'exploit' choice in the gamble the executives reactions above.

When a gamble the board methodology is endorsed by the fitting individual or gathering, draw up an activity plan and designate somebody to start to lead the pack on carrying out it.

4. RISK Observing

You've distinguished a gamble and chosen how to deal with it. Next you need to screen that the activity plan is set up and helped through successfully.

The venture chief or hazard supervisor ought to check in with risk proprietors consistently, so that progress can be observed. Activity plans can find opportunity to finish, so ensure everybody has practical assumptions regarding when it will be feasible to say a gamble is really overseen - or even shut. Ensure the gamble proprietor has sufficient opportunity to commit to dealing with the gamble and regulating the execution of the activity plan.

If this all sounds like an unknown dialect up to this point, it very well may be the ideal opportunity for a gamble the executives counseling administrations to assist with laying out a strong base for your group's interaction.

5. RISK Audit

At long last, as we found in the initial step, risk distinguishing proof is certainly not a limited time offer exertion. You ought to have your dangers under normal audit. On an undertaking, the venture supervisor and group meet to examine the gamble log. At a hierarchical level, the gamble administration cycle will figure out who surveys the general gamble profile and ensures that different strides of the gamble the board interaction are being done actually and in adherence to any appropriate gamble the executives norms.

At the point when you are assembling your gamble the board preparing plans and teaching the business about how risk the executives cycles will function in your association, consider whether one interaction will deal with a wide range of hazard. Preferably, you ought to make a smoothed out process that serves all business divisions and a wide range of chance, whether they are consistence, danger, opportunity or control gambles.

Obviously, there's much more about risk the executives that we haven't addressed here. You can likewise take a gander in danger nearness, triggers, and an entire host of different things including devices that bring a degree of strength and development to the manner in which your association handles risk through and through.

In any case, it begins with a straightforward cycle that can be utilized on hierarchical gamble and undertaking risk. From that point, you can create and develop the methodologies used to oversee risk until this cycle turns out to be natural and part of the texture of how the association runs.

Recognizing and Surveying Dangers

Given a key colleague has become sick, there might be an asset accessibility risk assuming there is nobody accessible or fit for supplanting that individual. There may likewise be an expense increment risk from attempting to source out a substitution without prior warning having existing colleagues stay at work past 40 hours with an end goal to finish project expectations on time. Subsequent stages to be taken ought to incorporate returning to the gamble ID process since interior changes have emerged partially through the task.

The distinguished dangers can be portrayed in a gamble breakdown structure or recorded in a gamble register. The previous would show a progressive construction ordering takes a chance as indicated by their source, while the last option would incorporate a posting of dangers as per risk sources, reactions, and classes.

It seems like gamble recognizable proof was just finished toward the start of the last venture. Since risk distinguishing proof is an iterative interaction, the cycle ought to be returned to as changes emerge during the undertaking. To guarantee the outcome of the following task, you could conceptualize and talk with various colleagues. It would be advantageous to have a conversation with individuals who were associated with the past venture to find out earlier hindrances experienced and distinguish current undertaking chances. It would likewise be valuable to consider any suitable existing gamble agendas and illustrations gained from finished projects.

What are the sorts of chance ID?

There are a wide range of types and techniques for risk recognizable proof, including conceptualizing, underlying driver examination, and SWOT investigation. Every strategy holds its own benefits and weaknesses, and the best technique to utilize will rely upon the task, association, and sorts of dangers.

What is the principal motivation behind risk ID?

The fundamental motivation behind risk recognizable proof is to distinguish gambles with that might actually influence a task or association and report their qualities. A constant interaction ought to be returned to all through the venture life cycle to guarantee that all potential dangers have been recognized.

What Is Hazard ID?

Envision yourself as a task director dealing with another site for your organization. Despite the fact that the undertaking is tiny, it's essential for you to complete an intensive gamble the executives examination to guarantee that the site is conveyed by a concurred cutoff time and at a concurred cost. Risk the board will guarantee that the center functionalities of the site will be conveyed and that the plan guidelines won't be compromised.

The gamble the board interaction on a task comprises of four stages:

- Risk ID
- Risk appraisal
- Risk reaction advancement, and
- Risk reaction control
- Risk distinguishing proof is the method involved with posting potential venture gambles and their qualities.

The consequences of hazard ID are regularly reported in a gamble register, which incorporates a rundown of recognized takes a chance alongside their sources, potential gamble reactions, and chance classes. This data is utilized for risk examination, which thusly will uphold making risk reactions. Distinguished dangers can likewise be implied in a liability breakdown structure, a progressive design used to order potential undertaking gambles by source.

However the significant work on risk distinguishing proof is generally finished in the start of a task, it's memorable's vital that risk ID is an iterative interaction; new dangers can be recognized all through the venture life cycle as the consequence of interior or outside changes to an undertaking.

Risk Distinguishing proof Reason

The job of chance ID is to produce a rundown of potential dangers that could adversely influence the association's capacity to accomplish its goals. It is critical to distinguish gambles early so they can be overseen really. The motivations behind the gamble recognizable proof interaction are to limit the adverse consequence of venture dangers, expand the positive effect of task valuable open doors, work on the possibilities of undertaking a good outcome, and give data to the second step of the gamble the board cycle known as chance investigation.

Significance of Chance Recognizable proof Interaction

There are a few significant components that assist with making the fundamental significance of the gamble ID process. A portion of these components include:

- It is the most important phase in the gamble the board cycle and sets the establishment for the wide range of various advances.

- It gives data that is utilized in risk appraisal to decide the probability and effect of dangers.
- It assists with focusing on takes a chance for additional examination and activity.
- It gives data that can be utilized to foster gamble reaction plans.

Risk Recognizable proof Models

It very well may be helpful to manage an instances of hazard recognizable proof to perceive how the cycle functions by and by.

An undertaking director is arranging another product improvement project. They utilize the conceptualizing technique for risk distinguishing proof and recognize the accompanying dangers:

- The prerequisite could change during the task
- The improvement group probably won't have sufficient experience
- The timetable could slip

- The venture might experience issues being finished on time

Since the dangers have been recognized, the undertaking supervisor can survey the probability and effect of each gamble.

Note:

Risk ID is the most common way of recognizing gambles with that might actually influence a venture or association and recording their particular qualities. It is the most vital phase in the gamble the board cycle and is significant for guaranteeing that dangers are appropriately distinguished and made due. The consequences of the gamble recognizable proof are utilized during the gamble examination, which is the second move toward the gamble the executives cycle. There are numerous significant reasons for risk recognizable proof including giving data to gamble with investigation, expanding the possibilities of a venture or association's prosperity, and limiting the expected adverse consequence of different dangers.

Reason

The goal of the gamble recognizable proof cycle is to guarantee that all potential task chances are distinguished. The procedures for managing these dangers will be conceived during later gamble the board steps.

A definitive motivation behind risk ID is to limit the adverse consequence of task hiccups and dangers and to boost the positive effect of undertaking potential open doors. Simply by recognizing gambles first can a task supervisor control the effect of a gamble on a venture. Consciousness of potential task gambles diminishes the quantity of astonishments during the undertaking conveyance and, accordingly, works on the possibilities of venture achievement, permitting the group to meet the time, timetable, and quality targets of the undertaking.

At long last, the reason for risk distinguishing proof is to give data to the subsequent stage of the gamble the board cycle: risk examination.

Proactive Moves toward Moderate Business Dangers

As people, we're accustomed to surveying chances; it's important for our endurance systems. Be that as it may, restricting gamble — likewise called risk moderation — influences whether a business makes due.

Envision a situation where business pioneers don't stop to ponder previous slip-ups or continually plunge into new open doors disregarding what they could mean for their business — this doesn't be sound supportable.

To really lessen risk inside an association, we really want to comprehend the various sorts of chance and how to forestall them. In this article, we'll cover the different sorts of dangers, share four gamble moderation systems, and tell you the best way to fabricate an arrangement to help you future-evidence your business.

What is risk alleviation?

Risk moderation is the act of diminishing the effect of expected gambles by fostering an arrangement to make due, dispose of, or limit misfortunes however much as could reasonably be expected. After administration makes and does the arrangement, they'll screen progress and survey whether they need to alter any activities.

Basically, risk relief portrays the strategies and procedures that bring risk levels down to an okay level for the business.

However it could feel enticing to take a page from another business' gamble the executives book, your arrangement will rely upon your novel business procedure.

Carving out opportunity to make a special gamble relief plan could be the distinction between keeping areas of strength for a with clients and missing out on business. We should take a gander at what you would need to accomplish when you moderate dangers.

For what reason do we moderate gamble?

Sadly, overlooking gamble factors won't make chances vanish, and moving forward without an arrangement might harm your primary concern. To this end risk relief is significant.

With a substantial arrangement with clear things to do, you can keep gambles from transforming into issues that go crazy or even forestall gambles through and through.

This not just conveys substantial advantages —, for example, keeping your business beneficial — however it likewise has elusive advantages, for example, assisting you with keeping a decent standing for security inside the business and keeping inner and outer partners blissful.

The last option is critical. In a new study, 66% of respondents said the volume and intricacy of dangers were close to their most significant level in 14 years for a wide range of associations, while short of what 33% depicted their gamble the board processes as full grown or hearty.

Those functional dangers can cost time, cash, and other important assets. Assuming partners feel the dangers are too high or misused, that could prompt a reshuffle in administration. So risk moderation is fundamental, however before you can foster an arrangement, you really want to understand what takes a chance with you can confront.

What are the kinds of hazard you might experience?

The dangers you face might vary from those of one more business or industry, taking care of various clients or clients. All things considered, a couple of normal dangers include:

Consistence risk — when an organization disregards outer or inner guidelines, guidelines, or norms, its standing or funds are in danger. Organizations might confront losing clients or paying a fine because of breaking consistence guidelines.

Legitimate gamble — a sort of consistence risk that happens when an organization disrupts the public authority's guidelines for organizations. Organizations confronting legitimate dangers could likewise become involved with costly claims.

Vital gamble — the consequence of an organization's defective business procedure or scarcity in that department.

Reputational risk — a gamble that can adversely influence the organization's standing or popular assessment. Reputational dangers can bring about benefit misfortunes and diminished certainty among organization investors.

Functional gamble — a work's everyday exercises might possibly deplete its benefits. Both inner frameworks and outside elements can cause functional dangers.

Numerous organizations arrange lattices by results and probability, similar to the one above. Recognizing which dangers you'll confront is the most vital move toward forestalling them. For the most part, there are a couple of sorts of chance moderation techniques you can use to safeguard your business.

What are the four gamble moderation techniques?

There are four normal gamble alleviation procedures: evasion, decrease, transaction, and acknowledgment.

Aversion
With a gamble evasion technique, you go to lengths to stay away from the gamble from happening. This might require compromising

different assets or methodologies to guarantee you're doing all that could be within reach to stay away from the gamble.

For instance, you might confront a gamble where you will not have the option to get done with a job for a significant undertaking because of an absence of trained professionals. To keep away from this gamble, you could employ various experts in the event that one became ill or wasn't accessible.

Obviously, employing more assets would remove a greater cut from the spending plan, so surveying the amount you can think twice about a significant stage in this procedure.

Decrease

With this moderation approach, whenever you've finished your gamble investigation, you would do whatever it may take to diminish the probability of a gamble occurring or the effect would it be a good idea for it happen.

Suppose your financial plan is tight, and there's a gamble you can't finish a specific task because of an absence of assets.

You can diminish the probability of that chance happening by proactively dealing with the costs reasonably affordable. In this situation, you could pick a less expensive choice for unrefined substances or decrease the task extension to finish it inside financial plan.

Transaction

Moving dangers implies passing the gamble outcome to an outsider. This might entail paying an insurance company to cover particular risks for certain organizations.

Risk transaction could likewise be composed into contracts with providers, reevaluating accomplices, or workers for hire. In the event that a task gets deferred anticipating a section or administration from an outer project worker, for example, the project worker could have to deal with damages for any deficiency of income the business causes.

Likewise, in the event that an organization has representatives or project workers from around the world, a worldwide consistence counselor can help backing and address the difficulties inborn to broadening tasks across various nations.

Acknowledgment

In conclusion, we have the acknowledgment technique, and that implies tolerating the gamble the way things are. Now and again, the chance of remuneration offsets the gamble, and it's more valuable over the long haul to take the risk.

It could likewise be that the likelihood of the gamble happening is negligible or the adverse consequence is minor. For things in this "Low" risk classification, a business could have a continuous methodology to acknowledge the gamble.

With risk acknowledgment, it's imperative to screen the gamble cautiously for any progressions to effect or probability of event. You may likewise need to continue to gauge the gamble against your gamble craving and evaluate whether worrying about the concern of hazard keeps on being the best move.

We've recognized various sorts of dangers and examined a few relief procedures. Presently, now is the right time to set the above in motion and perceive how you can relieve chances.

Commonsense advances you can take to relieve risk

Risk alleviation steps should be reasonable. It won't help your business on the off chance that you can't sort out some way to really moderate the dangers you're confronting.

The accompanying five stages will assist you with sorting out a way forward through your gamble moderation process. We should separate it.

1. Recognize

Prior to fostering any arrangement, you might need to recognize any gamble that could influence your undertaking or more extensive business activities. In this stage, it's critical to team up with a wide choice of partners with various business points of view to allow yourself the best opportunity of recognizing every single imaginable gamble.

For projects, project documentation can go about as a significant wellspring of data. Audit comparable undertakings for hints about potential dangers you could experience.

2. Survey

Presently you have a rundown of all your potential dangers, now is the right time to survey them by investigating the probability that they will happen and the level of adverse consequence your business would confront.

Your activities for each chance will rely upon which classification they fall into after your gamble appraisal. For instance, as referenced prior, you could choose to acknowledge all "Low" class gambles, decrease or move "Medium" gambles, and stay away from all "High" class chances.

3. Treat

Right now, you're settling on your alleviating activity and setting up methodologies. Try to record each gamble, its classification, and your picked counteraction estimates in a gamble register.

This is an asset for all partners to allude to and comprehend the arrangement and which moves to initiate if necessary. A gamble register will forestall disarray down the line, assisting your group with remaining coordinated and adjusted in the event that dangers happen.

4. Screen

Organizations aren't static and activities regularly change. It's fundamental to routinely screen each gamble to really look at its classification and alleviation procedure.

You can set up times in your week by week gatherings or day to day stand ups to survey gambles rapidly. You can likewise utilize a few factual devices —, for example, S-bends — to follow project progress and banner any progressions in the gamble profile for key factors, for example, project cost and length.

5. Report

Sharing data on chances, best practices, and moderation approaches can make your business' gamble alleviation system much more viable. Keeping takes a chance extremely important to partners is indispensable for informed direction, and normal revealing might surface different dangers that haven't been distinguished at this point.

The best alleviation methodologies make risk revealing piece of standard business activities by meshing it into the everyday or week after week work processes. One approach to effortlessly execute revealing is with the underlying announcing abilities and pre-fabricated risk the board formats.

CHAPTER 3:

Creative Solutions for Abundance Creation

Recognizing the Effect of Abundance and Its Impact

When it comes to financial matters, the concept of the abundance impact plays a big role in shaping financial decisions and outcomes. The abundance impact refers to the psychological and social shifts brought about by variations in wealth in consumer spending and saving behaviors. This oddity stems from the idea that people typically save more money when they feel unfortunate and spend more money when they feel wealthy. Because abundance has a significant impact on monetary development, monetary steadiness, and overall prosperity, it is essential knowledge for individuals, organizations, and policymakers alike.

1. The Mental Viewpoint: People often feel more confident and optimistic about their financial situation when they witness an increase in abundance, whether as a result of growing resource costs, wage growth, or other factors. As people realize they have more extra money to support their ideal way of life, this increase in confidence leads to a notable increase in the desire to spend and consume. Contrary to popular belief, a decrease in abundance can cause feelings of fear and vulnerability, causing people to tighten their purse strings and simplify their financial management strategies.

2. Purchaser Spending and Financial Development: The total impact of abundance influences buyer spending, which in turn propels financial development. People are likely to engage in optional spending when they feel wealthier, such as buying ostentatious goods, taking trips, or dining at posh restaurants. Increased consumer spending drives demand and compels businesses to produce more goods and labor, which spurs economic growth.

Conversely, in periods of diminishing wealth, consumers tend to reduce superfluous purchases, potentially impeding financial advancement.

3. Resource Cost Expansion: Particularly in the lodging and financial exchanges, the abundance impact is closely linked to resource cost expansion. When these resources appreciate in value, property owners and investors feel a wave of support that can spur increased spending and money movement. However, it is important to remember that, if not managed properly, resource value expansion can also result in theoretical air pockets and financial instability. For example, the 2008 real estate collapse was partially attributed to the burst of a hotel bubble, resulting in a sharp decline in wealth and a consequent adverse effect on abundance.

4. Strategy Suggestions: When making financial arrangements, policymakers often consider the impact of abundance. For instance, national banks may use expansionary money-related tactics, such as lowering loan costs or taking part in quantitative easing, during periods of economic downturn in order to stimulate resource costs and increase consumer spending. These steps aim to support financial recovery and have a positive abundance effect by encouraging people to spend more. Either way, it is imperative that policymakers find some sort of balance, since unwarranted increases in resource values can lead to monetary imbalances and financial instability.

5. The Best Option: Focusing on sustainable abundance creation and distribution is essential if we are to address the abundance impact and create a more promising future. More equitable and long-term abundance creation can result from promoting comprehensive monetary development, improving educational opportunities, and ensuring fair access to financial resources rather than relying solely on resource cost expansion, which can be erratic and prone to bubbles. Social orders can address the abundance impact in a more impartial and tenable manner by providing people with the tools and valuable opportunities to establish financial stability, while also attending to abundance differences.

In order to make educated decisions and influence financial outcomes, individuals, organizations, and policymakers must have a solid understanding of the abundance impact and its implications. We are much more likely to investigate the complexities of abundance creation if we are aware of the mental angles, the relationship between consumer spending and financial development, the task of resource cost expansion, and the approach recommendations. Finally, by focusing on the creation and distribution of reasonable abundance, we can outfit the abundance impact to create a more promising future for everybody.

Changing Perceptions to Advance

1. Acknowledging the Abundance Creation Attitude

It is imperative that we change our perspective and adopt a different one in order to fully realize the impact of abundance creation. This involves realizing that creating abundance involves more than just financial gain—it's also about self-awareness and fulfillment. By focusing on our perspective, we can overcome limiting beliefs and cultivate the adaptability and confidence necessary for advancement.

Understanding 1: Adopt a Mindset of Overflow

Having an overflow mindset is essential to creating abundance. This involves letting go of the fear-based worldview that is based on need and limitations and embracing the fact that there are enough opportunities for abundance and progress on the planet. Adopting an overflow mindset opens our doors to new opportunities and guarantees challenges that could lead to significant financial growth.

Knowledge 2: Take on a Development Outlook

A development outlook is one more urgent component in the brain research of abundance creation. This outlook underscores the conviction that our capacities and insight can be created through commitment and difficult work. By survey difficulties and misfortunes as any open doors for learning and development, we are bound to persist notwithstanding difficulty and eventually make more prominent progress.

2. Conquering Restricting Convictions

To move our attitude for abundance creation, we should initially recognize and defeat any restricting convictions that might be keeping us down. These convictions can go from self-uncertainty and anxiety toward inability to cultural assumptions and imbued ideas about cash. By testing and rethinking these convictions, we can prepare for a more prosperous future.

Understanding 1: Challenge Your Cash Contents

Cash scripts are the convictions and perspectives we hold about cash that shape our monetary way of behaving. It is essential to analyze these contents and decide if they are serving us or keeping us down. For instance, assuming we accept that cash is intrinsically underhanded or that we are not meriting abundance, we may unwittingly undermine our own monetary achievement. By testing and reexamining these contents, we can make new, enabling convictions that help our abundance creation venture.

Knowledge 2: Encircle Yourself with Positive Impacts

Our current circumstance and individuals we encircle ourselves with essentially affect our mentality. To develop an abundance creation mentality, it is critical to search out certain impacts and encircle ourselves with people who support our objectives and goals. By taking part in discussions and exercises that advance development and achievement, we can support our own confidence in our capacity to make riches.

3. Making a move and Creating Financial wellbeing

While mentality is essential, it is similarly critical to make a move and carry out systems that will prompt abundance creation. Here, we investigate various methodologies and choices for creating financial momentum, featuring the best techniques.

Knowledge 1: Putting resources into Resources

One method for creating financial momentum is through putting resources into resources that value over the long run. This could incorporate stocks, land, or organizations. By decisively assigning our assets and broadening our ventures, we can benefit from the influence of intensifying returns and produce significant abundance over the long haul.

Knowledge 2: Business venture and Undertakings

For those with an enterprising soul, beginning a business or wandering into business venture can be an exceptionally worthwhile way to abundance creation. By recognizing market holes and giving imaginative arrangements, business people have the chance to make esteem and create huge monetary returns. In any case, it is vital to painstakingly evaluate gambles and have a strong marketable strategy set up to guarantee a positive outcome.

Moving our mentality and embracing a brain research of abundance creation is essential for making long haul monetary progress. By embracing an overflow mentality, testing restricting convictions, and making an essential move, we can tackle the abundance impact and construct a more promising time to come for us and ages to come.

Procedures for Long haul Development

Creating Financial wellbeing through Ventures: procedures for Long haul development

Contributing is an incredible asset for creating financial wellbeing and getting a more promising time to come. It permits people to give their cash something to do and create returns over the long haul. In any case, fruitful money management requires cautious preparation and key direction. In this segment, we will investigate different methodologies for long haul development through speculations, giving experiences according to alternate points of view and contrasting various choices with assistance you settle on informed choices.

1. Enhancement: One significant technique for long haul development is differentiating your speculation portfolio. By spreading your ventures across various resource classes, businesses, and topographical districts, you can lessen the gamble related with any single speculation. For instance, rather than putting all your cash in one stock, consider differentiating by putting resources into a blend of stocks, bonds, land, and different resources. Along these lines, assuming one speculation performs ineffectively, others might counterbalance the misfortunes and give by and large development.

2. mitigating risk over time: minimizing risk is a technique that implies financial planning a proper measure of cash at normal spans, paying little mind to economic situations. This approach mitigates the effect of market unpredictability and eliminates the need to time the market. For example, on the off chance that you put $500 in a common asset consistently, you will purchase more offers when costs are low and less offers when costs are high. Over the long haul, this system can prompt critical long haul development, as it exploits market vacillations.

3. file reserves: Record reserves are a well known venture choice for long haul development. These assets plan to reproduce the presentation of a particular market list, like the S&P 500. By putting resources into list reserves, you gain openness to an expansive scope of organizations, enhancing your possessions and lessening risk. Besides, file reserves frequently have lower charges contrasted with effectively oversaw reserves, which can eat into your profits after some time. For instance, rather than putting resources into individual stocks, consider putting resources into a list reserve that tracks a deep rooted market file.

4. Land Speculation: Land can be an astounding long haul venture methodology for growing a strong financial foundation. It offers the potential for both capital appreciation and rental pay. Putting resources into investment properties can give a constant flow of income, while property estimations regularly value over the long run. Also, land ventures can offer expense benefits, for example, deterioration allowances and the capacity to concede capital additions charges through 1031 trades. In any case, it is fundamental to completely explore the market, area, and possible dangers prior to wandering into land ventures.

5. Retirement Records: Retirement accounts, for example, 401(k)s or IRAs, are explicitly intended for long haul development and establishing financial stability. These records offer expense benefits, for example, charge conceded or tax-exempt development, contingent upon the kind of record. By reliably adding to your retirement record and exploiting any business matching commitments, you can profit from intensifying returns over the long haul. Consider augmenting your commitments to retirement records to make the most of the tax cuts and speed up your drawn out abundance development.

6. Schooling and Information: Ultimately, putting resources into your own schooling and information about financial planning is critical for long haul development. The more you grasp different speculation choices, procedures, and market drifts, the better prepared you will be to settle on informed choices. Consider perusing speculation books, going to classes, or talking with monetary consultants to improve your venture information. By constantly learning and remaining informed, you can pursue better speculation decisions and augment your establishing a strong financial foundation potential.

Creating financial momentum through speculations requires cautious preparation and key navigation. By differentiating your portfolio, rehearsing mitigating risk, taking into account file reserves, investigating land speculations, using retirement records, and putting resources into your own insight, you can show yourself a way towards long haul development and monetary security. Keep in mind, every individual's conditions and chance resilience might fluctuate, so it is fundamental to evaluate your own monetary objectives and talk with experts prior to settling on any venture choices.

Opening the Force of Property Venture utilizing Land: Opening the Force of Property Venture

land has for quite some time been viewed as a rewarding speculation road, offering a large number of abundance creation open doors. Whether it's putting resources into private properties, business structures, or even empty land, the potential for critical returns is unquestionable. In this part, we will dig into the different manners by which land can be utilized to open the influence of property venture, investigating the advantages, systems, and potential entanglements that accompany this abundance creation road.

1. Rental Pay: One of the most well-known ways of utilizing land is through rental pay. Buying a property and leasing it out to occupants can give a constant flow of income, making it an appealing choice for financial backers looking for normal pay. Besides, investment properties have the potential for long haul appreciation, permitting financial backers to profit from both rental pay and capital increases. For instance, putting resources into a multi-unit apartment complex can create numerous floods of rental pay, expanding the general productivity of the speculation.

2. Fix and Flip: One more system for utilizing land is the fix and flip methodology. This includes buying a property that is needing redesigns, making the vital upgrades, and afterward selling it for a benefit. This technique requires a sharp eye for underestimated properties and the capacity to precisely gauge redesign costs. While fix and flip can be a high-risk, high-reward speculation methodology, it can yield significant returns whenever executed effectively. For example, buying a troubled property in a positive area, redesigning it to fulfill market needs, and selling it at a greater cost can bring about a huge benefit.

3. land Speculation trusts (REITs): For those searching for a more inactive way to deal with land venture, REITs offer an alluring choice. Organizations that own, labor, or finance the creation of land are known as REITs. By putting resources into REITs, people can acquire openness to a differentiated arrangement of properties without the requirement for direct possession. This choice gives liquidity, proficient administration, and the potential for customary pay through profits. Also, REITs offer the valuable chance to put resources into different sorts of land, like private, business, or modern, permitting financial backers to expand their portfolios and alleviate risk.

4. land crowdfunding: With the ascent of innovation, land crowdfunding has arisen as a famous method for utilizing property speculation. This involves combining resources from different investors to finance a real estate project. Crowdfunding stages give people the valuable chance to put resources into properties that might have in any case been distant because of high passage boundaries. Financial backers can look over a scope of ventures, like private turns of events, business properties, or even huge scope foundation projects. This choice considers broadening and possibly more significant yields contrasted with customary land venture roads.

5. Examination and Most ideal Choice: While considering the most ideal choice for utilizing land, it at last relies upon a singular's objectives, risk resistance, and accessible assets. Rental pay gives a consistent income and the potential for long haul appreciation, making it reasonable for those looking for ordinary pay and abundance gathering. Fix and flip, then again, offers the potential for easy gains however requires a more elevated level of mastery and inclusion. reits and land crowdfunding give inactive speculation amazing open doors the potential for enhancement and liquidity.

Land speculation can be a strong abundance creation device when utilized really. Whether through rental pay, fix and flip, REITs, or land crowdfunding, financial backers have a scope of choices to browse. It is pivotal to painstakingly assess every methodology, taking into account factors like gamble, return potential, and individual inclinations. By figuring out the complexities of land speculation and saddling its influence, people can construct a more promising time to come and open the abundance creation potential that property venture offers.

Facing Challenges for Independence from the rat race

Abundance Creation: Facing Challenges for Independence from the rat race

Business has for some time been viewed as a pathway to independence from the rat race, offering people the chance to make abundance through the quest for their own undertakings. It exemplifies the soul of proceeding with carefully thought out plans of action, frequently prompting astounding prizes. In the present steadily advancing economy, where conventional vocation ways are as of now not so secure as they used to be, business has turned into an undeniably appealing choice for those trying to create financial momentum and secure their monetary future.

1. The Force of Business:

Business permits people to assume command over their monetary predetermination, giving them the independence to set out their own open doors and shape their own prosperity. By recognizing holes on the lookout and offering inventive arrangements, business visionaries can possibly create significant abundance as well as have an enduring effect on society. Take, for instance, the example of overcoming adversity of Elon Musk, who established various organizations like Tesla and SpaceX, altering the auto and space businesses. His pioneering adventures have not just made him quite possibly of the richest person on the planet however have additionally prepared for progressions in manageable energy and space investigation.

2. Gambles with versus Rewards:

While business venture offers gigantic potential for abundance creation, it isn't without its dangers. beginning a business without any preparation requires a critical speculation of time, exertion, and capital. There is generally an opportunity of disappointment, and not all adventures will yield the ideal monetary results. In any case, it is essential to take note of that well balanced plans of action can frequently prompt significant prizes. For example, Imprint Zuckerberg removed a gamble by dropping from Harvard to zero in on creating Facebook. His bet paid off, and today he is one of the most youthful very rich people around the world, exhibiting the potential for exceptional accomplishment through pioneering pursuits.

3. Broadening and numerous Surges of pay:

Business visionaries frequently enjoy the benefit of expanding their revenue sources, which can additionally improve their abundance creation potential. By laying out various organizations or putting resources into various endeavors, business people can moderate the dangers related with depending on a solitary type of revenue. For example, Richard Branson, the organizer behind Virgin Gathering, has broadened his business domain across different ventures, including avionics, music, and media communications. This enhancement methodology has permitted him to collect significant abundance as well as furnished him with a security net in the event that one area encounters a slump.

4. Putting resources into Existing Organizations versus Beginning Without any preparation:

Business doesn't be guaranteed to require beginning a business without any preparation. Another choice is to put resources into existing organizations or get establishments. This approach permits people to use the demonstrated outcome of laid out brands while as yet partaking in the advantages of business. For instance, rather than beginning another eatery idea, one could put resources into an establishment like Mcdonald's, profiting from a laid out brand, functional frameworks, and a demonstrated history of progress. While this choice might require a higher introductory speculation, it might possibly give a safer way to abundance creation.

5. Building an Organization and Coordinated efforts:

One urgent part of business venture is building areas of strength for an and looking for coordinated efforts. By encircling themselves with similar people and industry specialists, business visionaries can acquire significant experiences, access new open doors, and tap into a more extensive client base. Joint effort with different business visionaries or organizations can prompt commonly advantageous associations, empowering business visionaries to use each other's assets and assets. For instance, organizations between innovation new businesses and laid out enterprises have become progressively normal, permitting new companies to get to financing and skill while furnishing laid out organizations with inventive arrangements.

Business venture presents a strong road for people to make riches and accomplish independence from the rat race. While it implies facing challenges, the potential prizes can be significant. Whether beginning a business without any preparation, enhancing revenue sources, or putting resources into existing endeavors, there are different ways to seek after business. By embracing the enterprising outlook, people can saddle the abundance impact and fabricate a more promising time to come for them as well as their networks.

1. The significance of training in abundance creation couldn't possibly be more significant. Training outfits people with the information and abilities important to explore the intricate universe of money, speculations, and business. It engages people to pursue informed choices, immediately take advantage of chances, and successfully deal with their assets. According to a cultural viewpoint, a knowledgeable populace cultivates financial development, advancement, and social versatility. Notwithstanding, the job of schooling in abundance creation goes past getting monetary proficiency; it envelops self-improvement, decisive reasoning, and the capacity to adjust to an always changing financial scene.

2. Putting resources into formal instruction is in many cases the most vital move towards abundance creation. Chasing after advanced education, like a professional education or particular confirmations, gives people serious areas of strength for an of information in their picked fields. This can open ways to worthwhile vocation open doors, higher acquiring potential, and expanded employer stability. Moreover, instruction imparts discipline, determination, and a solid hard working attitude, which are fundamental characteristics for making long haul monetary progress.

3. Past conventional schooling, people can likewise put resources into self-instruction through nonstop learning and improvement. This can be accomplished through understanding books, going to workshops, taking part in web-based courses, or looking for mentorship from fruitful people in their separate fields. Self-schooling permits people to remain refreshed with industry patterns, obtain new abilities, and expand their insight base. For example, somebody intrigued by land money management can teach themselves about market patterns, property valuation procedures, and exchange systems to settle on informed venture choices.

4. One more road for putting resources into training is through business and beginning a business. Business expects people to continually learn and adjust to stay serious on the lookout. By putting resources into their very own and proficient development, business people can improve their business insight, foster initiative abilities, and gain a more profound comprehension of their objective market. This information can be instrumental in building an effective business and creating riches.

5. Taking into account the money saving advantage investigation of different instructive options is significant. While seeking after advanced education at esteemed foundations might offer important systems administration valuable open doors and admittance to top-level assets, it frequently accompanies a heavy sticker price. On the other hand, people can investigate more reasonable choices like junior colleges, online courses, or professional preparation programs that give specific abilities applicable to their ideal vocation ways. At last, the most ideal choice relies upon a singular's objectives, monetary conditions, and the particular business they wish to enter.

6. Finally, recognizing the job of experiential learning in abundance creation is pivotal. While instruction gives areas of strength for an establishment, commonsense experience is similarly significant. Temporary positions, apprenticeships, and active undertakings permit people to apply their insight in genuine situations, gain industry-explicit abilities, and fabricate an expert organization. For instance, somebody inspired by the financial exchange can begin just barely of cash and gaining from their triumphs and disappointments.

All in all, schooling assumes a significant part in abundance creation by furnishing people with the essential information, abilities, and mentality to flourish in a serious monetary scene. Putting resources into instruction, whether through formal or self-schooling, business, or experiential learning, opens ways to open doors, improves procuring potential, and cultivates self-awareness. At last, the decision of instructive way ought to be founded on individual objectives, monetary contemplations, and the particular business one wishes to enter. By putting resources into information, people can outfit the force of training to construct a more splendid and more prosperous future.

Securing and Developing Your Resources

Abundance Conservation: Securing and Developing Your Resources

In the present steadily changing monetary scene, it has become progressively vital to make abundance as well as safeguard it. Abundance protection includes defending your well deserved resources from likely dangers and guaranteeing their development after some time. By taking on a proactive way to deal with abundance conservation, people can get their monetary future and fabricate a strong starting point for a more splendid tomorrow.

1. Broaden Your Portfolio: One of the basic standards of abundance safeguarding is expansion. Spreading your speculations across various resource classes, like stocks, bonds, land, and products, can assist with alleviating gambles and augment returns. By expanding, you decrease the effect of any single speculation's terrible showing on your general portfolio. For instance, a decrease in the securities exchange might be balanced by gains in land or bonds, saving your riches.

2. Put resources into Protection: Protection assumes a vital part in abundance conservation by giving security against unanticipated occasions. Health care coverage, extra security, and property protection are fundamental parts of a far reaching abundance safeguarding system. These strategies defend your resources and offer monetary help in the midst of health related crises, catastrophic events, or appalling occasions. By putting resources into protection, you can safeguard your abundance and guarantee that it stays in salvageable shape in any event, during testing times.

3. Home Preparation: making arrangements for what's in store is crucial with regards to abundance protection. Domain arranging permits you to decide how your resources will be dispersed after your passing, guaranteeing that your abundance is saved for people in the future. By making a will, laying out trusts, and assigning recipients, you can shield your resources from superfluous charges, legitimate debates, and other likely dangers. Domain arranging likewise gives a valuable chance to help causes or good cause that are near your heart, leaving an enduring inheritance.

4. Look for Proficient Direction: Abundance conservation can be perplexing, and looking for proficient counsel is pivotal to explore through the complexities of monetary preparation. Talking with a monetary counsel or abundance director can give significant experiences and systems customized to your particular necessities and objectives. These experts can assist you with surveying your gamble resistance, foster a money growth strategy, and recognize valuable open doors for development. Their skill and experience can direct you towards the most ideal choices for saving and developing your riches.

5. Think about Elective Speculations: While conventional ventures like stocks and bonds have their benefits, investigating elective venture choices can offer extra roads for abundance safeguarding. For example, putting resources into land, confidential value, or investment can give broadening and potential returns not associated with the securities exchange. Via cautiously assessing these other options and taking into account their gamble reward profiles, you can recognize chances to safeguard and develop your resources past customary venture roads.

6. Remain Informed and Adjust: The monetary scene is continually developing, and remaining informed about market patterns, administrative changes, and financial movements is fundamental for compelling abundance safeguarding. By watching out for the market, you can go with informed choices and adjust your speculation procedures as needs be. Consistently looking into and rebalancing your portfolio guarantees that it lines up with your changing monetary objectives and hazard craving.

Abundance safeguarding is an imperative part of building a more promising time to come. By expanding your portfolio, putting resources into protection, taking part in domain arranging, looking for proficient direction, taking into account elective ventures, and remaining informed, you can safeguard and develop your resources actually. Keep in mind, abundance safeguarding requires a proactive methodology and a drawn out mentality. With cautious preparation and vital direction, you can shield your riches and appreciate monetary security into the indefinite future.

Utilizing Abundance to Have a Beneficial outcome on Society

Offering back is a fundamental piece of abundance creation. As people gather riches, they have the influence to have a constructive outcome on society by using their assets to help causes and drives that line up with their qualities. This segment dives into the different manners by which people can utilize their abundance to offer in return, featuring the significance of altruism and socially capable money management.

1. Charity: Quite possibly of the most well-known way people offer back is through altruism. By giving cash, assets, or time to beneficent associations, people can straightforwardly uphold causes that are mean a lot to them. Charity permits people to have an unmistakable effect in the existences of others and add to the improvement of society. For instance, extremely rich person donor Bill Doors has devoted a critical part of his abundance to handling worldwide issues like neediness, medical care, and instruction through the Bill and Melinda Entryways Establishment.

2. Influence Money management: One more way to deal with offering back is through influence effective financial planning. This involves putting resources into organizations, associations, or assets that expect to create both monetary returns and positive social or natural results. Influence effective money management empowers people to adjust their speculation portfolio to their qualities and make a twofold main concern monetary and social returns. For example, putting resources into environmentally friendly power projects gives monetary returns as well as adds to alleviating environmental change and advancing manageability.

3. Corporate Social obligation (CSR): Organizations likewise assume a urgent part in rewarding society. Through CSR drives, organizations add to the prosperity of their networks and address social and ecological difficulties. This can incorporate drives, for example, worker volunteer projects, ecological maintainability endeavors, or gifts to admirable missions. For instance, the open air clothing organization Patagonia is known for its obligation to natural activism, giving a level of its deals to ecological associations and supporting grassroots natural missions.

4. social business: social business joins business standards with an emphasis on resolving social or natural issues. Social business people make imaginative answers for cultural issues, frequently through the foundation of social endeavors. These undertakings expect to produce feasible income while at the same time making a positive effect on society. For example, TOMS Shoes spearheaded the "One for One" model, where for each sets of shoes sold, a couple is given to a youngster out of luck.

5. Training and Ability building: Putting resources into instruction and expertise building programs is one more method for offering in return. By furnishing people with admittance to quality schooling and preparing open doors, abundance makers can engage others to work on their lives and add to society. Grants, mentorship programs, and professional preparation drives are only a couple of instances of how people can uphold training and expertise building endeavors.

While considering the most ideal choice for offering in return, it is vital to assess individual qualities, assets, and the likely effect of each methodology. A few people might decide to zero in on one explicit road, while others might favor a mix of approaches. Eventually, the most ideal choice is one that lines up with a singular's interests, esteems, and wanted influence on society. By tackling their abundance to have a beneficial outcome, people have the chance to make a more promising time to come for them and others.

Embracing the Abundance Impact for a More promising time to come

The abundance impact is a peculiarity that has been broadly considered and bantered among financial specialists and monetary specialists. It alludes to the effect of changes in the worth of resources, like stocks, land, and different speculations, on shopper spending and in general monetary development. The idea recommends that when people see themselves to be richer because of an expansion in resource values, they are bound to spend and contribute, subsequently animating monetary movement.

One point of view on embracing the abundance impact is that it can prompt expanded purchaser certainty and spending, which thusly drives monetary development. At the point when people see their speculations and resources fill in esteem, they have a good sense of safety and are more ready to make buys and ventures. This expanded spending spurs interest for labor and products, prompting position creation and by and large monetary extension.

Nonetheless, pundits contend that depending too intensely on the abundance impact can make a misguided feeling of flourishing and add to monetary unsteadiness. They battle that when resource values are misleadingly expanded, for example, during a speculative air pocket, the ensuing blasting of the air pocket can prompt extreme monetary slumps. This was clear in the 2008 monetary emergency, where the breakdown of the real estate market and ensuing decrease in resource values devastatingly affected the worldwide economy.

In spite of these worries, there are ways of outfitting the abundance impact for a more promising time to come while relieving the dangers. Here are a few choices to consider:

1. Differentiate ventures: Rather than depending entirely on one resource class, like land or stocks, expand your portfolio to spread the gamble. By putting resources into a blend of stocks, bonds, land, and different resources, you can lessen the effect of an expected slump in any one area.

2. Put resources into useful resources: As opposed to exclusively zeroing in on theoretical speculations, consider putting resources into resources that produce pay or have natural worth. This could incorporate investment properties, profit paying stocks, or organizations that give fundamental labor and products. By putting resources into useful resources, you might not just advantage from expected capital appreciation at any point yet additionally produce progressing pay.

3. Save and contribute as long as possible: It's critical to have a drawn out viewpoint with regards to abundance creation. Rather than attempting to time the market or pursue momentary additions, center around saving and contributing reliably after some time. This approach permits you to profit from intensifying returns and diminishes the effect of transient market changes.

4. Focus on monetary training: To go with informed venture choices, having a strong comprehension of monetary ideas and strategies is fundamental. Find opportunity to instruct yourself about various venture choices, risk the board, and individual accounting. This information will engage you to go with better monetary choices and explore the intricacies of the abundance impact.

Embracing the abundance impact can have both positive and negative ramifications for people and the economy all in all. By broadening ventures, zeroing in on useful resources, putting something aside as long as possible, and focusing on monetary schooling, people can tackle the abundance impact for a more promising time to come while limiting the dangers related with resource bubbles and financial shakiness. It means quite a bit to work out some kind of harmony between partaking in the advantages of expanded riches and keeping a judicious way to deal with monetary preparation and navigation.

Utilizing Innovation for Benefit

In the quickly developing scene of business, the essential usage of innovation has turned into a critical driver for benefit expansion. This article investigates the extraordinary job of innovation in improving functional productivity, upgrading client commitment, and opening new income streams. By bridling the force of creative advances, organizations can smooth out their cycles as well as position themselves for supported development and productivity.

Upgrading Functional Productivity

Innovative headways offer organizations a variety of devices to smooth out tasks and increment productivity. Computerization of routine errands, execution of information examination, and the reception of cloud-based arrangements can fundamentally decrease functional expenses and improve efficiency. By utilizing innovation to improve work processes, organizations make a less fatty and more spry functional system, eventually adding to higher net revenues.

Upgrading Client Commitment

Innovation gives remarkable open doors to organizations to draw in with clients in significant ways. From customized promoting procedures driven by information examination to intelligent client support stages, organizations can make a consistent and vivid client experience. Connected with clients are bound to make rehash buys and become brand advocates, straightforwardly affecting the primary concern and adding to supported productivity.

Opening New Income Streams

Advancement in innovation opens roads for organizations to investigate and exploit new income streams. The ascent of web based business, membership based models, and advanced administrations embody how innovation can change customary plans of action. By embracing these progressions and decisively coordinating innovation into income age systems, organizations can take advantage of developing business sectors and profit by advancing shopper patterns.

Methodologies for Execution

1. Putting resources into Information Investigation: Outfitting the force of information through examination permits organizations to settle on informed choices, distinguish market patterns, and target explicit client fragments, adding to additional powerful and productive techniques.

2. Embracing Cloud-Based Arrangements: Cloud innovation gives adaptability, adaptability, and cost-adequacy. Taking on cloud-based arrangements can upgrade functional proficiency, lessen IT framework costs, and add to generally speaking benefit amplification.

3. Embracing Internet business and Advanced Stages: The computerized commercial center offers immense open doors for income age. Organizations ought to decisively embrace internet business stages, advanced commercial centers, and other web-based channels to grow their span and drive deals.

4. Putting resources into Development: Remaining ahead in the innovation scene requires a guarantee to advancement. Organizations ought to dispense assets to innovative work, encouraging a culture that embraces arising advancements and investigates novel answers for industry challenges.

In a period where innovation is a main impetus behind business development, utilizing imaginative arrangements is as of now not a choice however an essential objective. Organizations that outfit innovation to advance activities, improve client commitment, and open new income streams are better situated for supported benefit expansion. The joining of innovation smoothes out current cycles as well as opens ways to phenomenal open doors, guaranteeing an upper hand in the present unique business climate.

Innovative Income Streams

Creative Revenue Sources: Propelling Compensation Age for Progress

In the current novel business scene, the journey for creative revenue streams is critical for upheld accomplishment. This guide researches innovative systems that individuals and associations can embrace to grow their compensation sources and conform to changing business area components.

Understanding Imaginative Revenue Sources

Inventive revenue streams go past customary compensation sources, offering innovative approaches to creating pay. The accentuation is on using inventiveness, imagination, and adaptability to uncover open entryways.

Portraying Inventive Revenue Sources: Emptying the thought and emphasizing that creative mind remembers innovative thinking for how pay is delivered.
The Adjustment of Business Guidelines: Seeing the changing thought of game plans and the necessity for aptitude and creative mind.
The Occupation of Adaptability: Highlighting the meaning of adaptability in perceiving and profiting from emerging entryways.

Using Existing Assets

Creative revenue streams incorporate reevaluating and enlarging existing assets. This portion explores procedures for isolating regard in view of what's at this point set up.

Adjusting Safeguarded development: Researching approaches to adjusting authorized advancement, for instance, approving, enhancing, or selling insightful assets.

Asset Reusing: Breaking down how associations can reuse existing things, organizations, or content to deal with new business areas or address emerging issues.

Agreeable Undertakings: Diving into the ability of joint endeavors and relationship to utilize combined resources and expertise.

Embracing the High level Economy

Inventive revenue streams much of the time incorporate handling the power of advancement and online stages. This portion researches streets inside the electronic space.

Online business Progressions: Researching innovative web plans of action, from enrollment based organizations to facilitate to-client bargains techniques.

Mechanized Things and Organizations: Examining the creation and variation of cutting edge things and organizations, for instance, online courses, computerized books, and high level craftsmanship.

The Gig Economy: Discussing how individuals can exploit the gig economy to offer their capacities or organizations on stages like rethinking destinations.

Profiting from Examples and Creating Business areas

Viable compensation age incorporates staying responsive to publicize designs and proactively acquiring by emerging entryways. This part covers.

Perceiving Examples: Methods for staying informed about industry designs, purchaser tendencies, and creating business areas.

Specialty Market Examination: The capacity of specialty markets and how associations can fit things or organizations to meet the outstanding prerequisites of express customer segments.

Early Gathering Advantage: The potential gains of being an early adopter of emerging progressions or strategies.

Adjusting Individual Stamping and Expertise

Individuals can foster creative revenue streams by adjusting their inclination. This section examines.

Building a Singular Brand: Methods for spreading out significant solid areas for a brand that attracts open entryways for talking responsibility, upholds, and composed endeavors.

Content Transformation: Using content creation to deliver pay through sponsorships, publicizing, and partner promoting.

Guiding and Preparing: Researching streets for offering directing or educating organizations considering individual capacity.

Reasonable and Socially Trustworthy Revenue Sources

In the hour of perceptive commercialization, associations are examining revenue streams that line up with reasonability and social commitment. This fragment covers.

Eco-obliging Things and Organizations: The climb of eco-discerning industrialism and methods for making and advancing legitimate things or organizations.

Corporate Social Commitment (CSR): The fuse of socially skilled crashes into game plans.

Impact Cash the board: Researching the ability of impact viable monetary preparation, where associations change financial targets to positive social or regular outcomes.

Inventive Supporting Models

Creative revenue streams can incorporate imaginative supporting models. This fragment explores.

Crowdfunding: The use of crowdfunding stages to raise capital for exercises, things, or drives.

Participation Models: The usage of enrollment based pay models for a steady progression of pay through rehashing portions.

Pay Sharing and Sways: Researching pay sharing game plans or prominence structures as elective supporting models.

Beating Troubles in Creative Pay Age

While inventive revenue streams offer stimulating possible results, they go with their game plan of troubles. This part watches out for ordinary snags and gives systems to vanquishing them.

Risk Easing: Procedures for recognizing and directing perils related with innovative revenue sources.

Adaptability: The meaning of flexibility in noting changing financial circumstances and refining creative pay frameworks.

Legal and Regulatory Considerations: Investigating authentic and authoritative designs while executing unique pay models.

The Possible destiny of Creative Revenue Sources: In imaginative revenue streams incorporate overhauling the case all around. From using existing assets for embracing modernized improvements and acquiring by emerging examples, associations and individuals that embrace creative mind, flexibility, and an earth shattering mindset are decisively positioned to prosper in this strong environment.

CHAPTER 4:

Shrewd Speculations: Exploring the Monetary Scene

In the complex and reliably creating universe of cash, making splendid endeavors is an establishment for making and safeguarding monetary solidness. This intensive associate intends to give pieces of information into investigating the financial scene insightfully. From understanding the basics of cash the executives to exploring different endeavor vehicles and strategies, this guide covers a scope of subjects to draw in individuals with the data expected to make taught and crucial hypothesis decisions.

Moreover

Contributing can be a useful asset for creating financial stability and getting monetary fates. Notwithstanding, the universe of speculations can be complicated and overpowering for the individuals who are new to the game. In this article, it'll investigate savvy venture tips to assist you with exploring the monetary scene with certainty.

Grasping Gamble Resilience

Prior to plunging into the huge expanse of venture choices, understanding your gamble tolerance is fundamental. This is the degree of hazard you are open to taking with your ventures.

Enhancement Techniques

"Try not to tie up your resources in one place" is a maxim that turns out as expected in the realm of ventures. Broadening is a system that includes spreading your speculations across various resources for decrease risk.

Investigating Venture Choices

Information is power, particularly in the domain of speculations. Set aside some margin to completely explore potential speculation choices.

Long haul versus Transient Speculations
Could it be said that you are in it for the long stretch or searching for speedy returns? Understanding the distinctions between long haul and transient speculations is essential.

Watching out for Market Patterns
The monetary business sectors are dynamic, and remaining informed about market patterns is critical to settling on informed venture choices.

The Force of Compounding
Albert Einstein once alluded to accumulate interest as the eighth marvel of the world. Understanding and saddling the influence of compounding can fundamentally affect your abundance over the long run.

Putting resources into Resources with Inborn Worth
While market patterns can be captivating, putting resources into resources with natural value is significant. Understanding the basics of

your speculations is fundamental for long haul achievement.

Adjusting to Monetary Changes

Monetary circumstances can impact speculation execution. Monitoring financial changes and changing your speculation systems appropriately is vital.

Putting forth Reasonable Objectives

Laying out clear and feasible speculation objectives gives a guide to your monetary excursion. Adjust your objectives to your gamble resilience and time skyline.

The Job of Crisis Assets

Contributing isn't just about making gains; it's likewise about safeguarding yourself from unanticipated conditions. Lay out and keep up with crisis assets for monetary dependability.

Charge Proficient Financial planning

Understanding the expense ramifications of your ventures is essential. Investigate charge proficient speculation procedures to augment your profits inside legitimate systems.

Constant Learning and Variation

The monetary scene is always advancing. Remain informed, look for continuous training, and be prepared to adjust to changes on the lookout and monetary guidelines.

Checking and Assessing Ventures

Whenever you've contributed, the excursion doesn't end. Lay out a daily practice for checking and assessing your ventures, and be ready to make changes depending on the situation

Savvy financial planning is an excursion that requires information, tolerance, and versatility. By figuring out your gamble resistance, expanding your ventures, and remaining informed, you can explore the monetary scene with certainty.

Figuring out Speculation Open doors

you the best insight of our Site. By utilizing our Site you are consenting to our utilization of treats.

Find out More

Abundance Academy™

You are here:Home/Effective money management/Figuring out Venture Open doors Effective money management

Figuring out Speculation Potential open doors

Various methods of Venture

In exceptionally straightforward terms, 'speculation open doors' allude to the roads that you can use to put away your extra money. There are a wide range of sorts of venture potential open doors accessible, contingent upon your gamble hunger and your comprehension of the different speculation instruments.

Here and there, individuals put resources into instruments that are connected with their own advantages. For instance, fine arts may not be ordinary venture valuable chances to a great many people however to the individuals who comprehend this market, it might possibly go out to worthwhile speculations.

In the following segment, I will investigate the different speculation amazing chances to all individuals.

Financial exchange

Chances are, you presumably have known about putting resources into the securities exchange or perhaps, you have even put before in stocks.

Basically, the securities exchange is a 'business opportunity' for financial backers/merchants to trade loads of public corporations. These days, trading should be possible electronically through a tick of a button.

In most evolved nations, there are laid out stock trades for financial backers to trade their stocks. In Singapore for instance, financial backers exchange stocks through the Singapore Stock Trade. In some cases, financial backers are additionally permitted to purchase stocks that are exchanged the stock trades of different nations.

For the vast majority, putting resources into the financial exchange is one of the most regular ways for them to contribute, since it is generally open to a great many people and financial exchange news is broadly plugged in many medias.

However stock costs truly do will generally move couple with the basic organizations' essentials over the long haul, in the short run, factors, for example, request and supply will generally impact the transient value development of stocks.

One of the keys to putting effectively in the securities exchange is to have the option to recognize winning loads of productive organizations which are displaying good cost activity designs.

Money

Another normal venture instrument that is getting more famous is that of cash exchanging or Forex (Unfamiliar Trade) exchanging. Forex exchanging is basically trading a nation's money, contingent upon whether you accept the worth of the cash would rise or fall.

Contrasted with the securities exchange, the money market is possibly more unpredictable and the volume of exchanging is higher. Dissimilar to the securities exchange, the cash market is open for exchanging all day, every day, during the work days.

One critical distinction between putting resources into stocks and Forex is that most Forex agents will generally offer more influence for retail financial backers. Like most cases, influence is possibly a situation with two sides and it is firmly fitting that you practice an expected level of effort prior to putting resources into any utilized instruments.

Product

You likely could have known about financial backers exchanging gold. Notwithstanding, gold is only one of the instruments accessible for exchanging the products market. A portion of the more normal wares exchanged incorporate valuable metals like gold and silver, raw petroleum and, surprisingly, farming produces, like wheat and sugar.

Nations, for example, Russia, Brazil and the Center East that are wealthy in item saves, are probably the most effectively exchanged habitats for wares. Nonetheless, product exchanging is likewise directed internationally through a wide organization of merchants, intermediaries and financial backers.

However there is a high volume of exchanging the wares market, this venture opportunity is prevalently a road for prepared financial backers, and it isn't utilized widely by new financial backers.

Bonds, Fixed Pay

Government and corporate security and, depositories are one of the venture instruments that are generally utilized by generally expert and retail financial backers across the world.

At the point when you put resources into an obligation of an organization for instance, you are basically crediting cash to the organization. Consequently, the organization will pay you interest routinely and when the bond develops (which is generally expressed when the bond is given), the organization will take care of you the head or the sum that was credit initially.

The prominence in bond ventures originates from the possibility that bonds are promoted as 'okay' instruments. To be sure, contrasted with stock costs, bond costs will more often than not be less unpredictable in for the most part. A few financial backers likewise really like to put resources into bonds principally due to they get a constant flow of pay (from the interest installments).

In a few created nations, for example, Singapore, bonds speculations are effectively open to retail financial backers.

Land

Financial backers putting resources into land, frequently do as such for several reasons. A few financial backers put resources into land to partake in the recurring, automated revenue from the rentals they gather routinely. Others put resources into land, essentially on the grounds that they accept the land will see the value in esteem after some time.

In certain nations, financial backers can exceptionally utilized their land speculations. Furthermore, as most utilized speculations, it might actually help them out by amplifying their profits or it could without much of a stretch crash the worth of their ventures.

Not at all like to the securities exchange, land speculations are by and large less fluid (for example you can't buy or a sell a piece of property rapidly) and land exchanges will generally take time.

Overseen Assets

A few financial backers like to designate putting away by stopping their cash with speculation supports that are overseen by reserve chiefs in light of the fact that these financial backers might have restricted opportunity to deal with their ventures.

There are a wide choice of speculation finances accessible in the market today. A few assets put resources into more 'okay' instruments, for example, bonds and fixed pay while some might put resources into 'higher gamble' instruments like new businesses.

Prior to putting resources into any oversaw reserves, you might need to think about whether your gamble craving is harmonious with that of the speculation store, the verifiable exhibition of the asset as well as the expenses related with putting resources into the assets.

Fine art, Collectibles

This maybe is one of the most whimsical venture open doors accessible and if might possibly produce extremely worthwhile returns assuming you comprehend the market well.

One thing to note however is that the market for whimsical ventures may not be as enormous or as fluid as regular instruments like the financial exchange. Consequently, it may not be simple for the proprietor of a piece of work of art for instance, to promptly track down a purchaser. In this way, conceivable proprietor's money could be 'secured' in the piece of work of art for quite a while.

Settling on Informed Monetary Choices

In the present complicated and speedy monetary business sectors, going with informed choices is critical for people and organizations the same. The capacity to accumulate, dissect, and decipher data really can mean the distinction among progress and disappointment in the realm of money. In this article, I will investigate the critical variables and systems that can assist you with pursuing informed choices in the monetary business sectors.

The Job of Data in Monetary Business sectors

Data is the soul of monetary business sectors. It drives the dynamic cycle and impacts the way of behaving of market members. Without admittance to precise and opportune data, pursuing informed choices in finance would be almost unthinkable. Data can emerge out of different sources, including fiscal summaries, financial reports, news stories, and master examination.

To go with informed monetary choices, taking into account the accompanying key factors is significant:

1. Precision: Guarantee that the data you depend on is exact and solid. Confirm the sources and cross-reference the information whenever the situation allows. Mistaken or deluding data can prompt unfortunate navigation and critical monetary misfortunes.

2. Pertinence: Assess the importance of the data to your particular monetary objectives and targets. Not all data is similarly helpful in each circumstance. Center around get-together information that is straightforwardly connected with your speculation system or monetary choice.

3. Idealness: Monetary business sectors are profoundly powerful, and data can immediately become obsolete. remain refreshed with the most recent news and improvements that might influence your monetary choices. Act quickly on time-delicate chances to boost your likely gains.

4. Amount: Don't over-burden yourself with a lot of data. Become amazing at sifting through clamor and zeroing in on the most applicable information. An excessive amount of data can prompt examination loss of motion and prevent your dynamic interaction.

Key Variables to Think about Prior to Settling on Monetary Choices

With regards to pursuing monetary choices, there are a few key factors that ought to be painstakingly thought of. These elements can shift contingent upon the particular circumstance, yet a few normal ones include:

1. Risk craving: Survey your capacity to bear risk prior to going with any monetary choices. Decide the amount you will lose and how much potential return you look for. This will assist you with picking fitting venture techniques and resources.

2. Monetary objectives: Obviously characterize your monetary objectives and targets. Whether you are putting something aside for retirement, purchasing a house, or beginning a business, having an unmistakable vision of what you need to accomplish will direct your dynamic interaction.

3. time skyline: Consider your time skyline for accomplishing your monetary objectives. transient objectives might require a more safe methodology, while long haul objectives might take into consideration higher gamble and possible returns.

4. Economic situations: Assess the ongoing economic situations and patterns that might influence your monetary choices. Consider factors, for example, loan costs, expansion, and market opinion. These variables can impact the exhibition of resources and the general economy.

5. Administrative climate: Know about the administrative climate that applies to your monetary choices. consistence with regulations and guidelines is essential for keeping away from legitimate issues and safeguarding your resources.

The Effect of Information Examination on Dynamic in Money
Influence Information

Information examination assumes a huge part in informed dynamic in finance. By investigating at various times information, monetary experts can draw significant bits of knowledge and make expectations about future market patterns. information examination methods and apparatuses have enormously developed as of late, offering more modern method for grasping monetary business sectors.

Here are a few key ways information examination can affect dynamic in finance:

1. Distinguishing designs: Information examination considers the ID of repeating examples and patterns in monetary business sectors. By concentrating on authentic information, market members can acquire experiences into market conduct and make more educated expectations.

2. Surveying risk: Information examination helps in evaluating chance and creating risk the board techniques. By investigating authentic unpredictability and relationships, financial backers can all the more likely comprehend the potential dangers related with their ventures.

3. Making expectations: Information examination can empower prescient displaying, which can be utilized to gauge market developments and settle on more precise venture choices. Procedures, for example, relapse examination and time series determining can give important expectations.

4. Portfolio streamlining: Information examination helps in enhancing speculation portfolios by distinguishing the ideal assignment of resources. By dissecting the presentation and connections of various resources, financial backers can accomplish a harmony among chance and return.

An illustration of the effect of information examination on dynamic in money should be visible in algorithmic exchanging. Using modern information examination strategies, algorithmic brokers can handle tremendous measures of information progressively to go with computerized exchanging choices. This type of exchanging depends intensely on information examination to recognize designs and execute exchanges at the most great costs.

Techniques for Social event and Assessing Monetary Data

Assembling and assessing monetary data is a critical stage in going with informed choices. Here are some systems to think about:

1. Broaden data sources: Depending on a solitary wellspring of data can be dangerous. Expand your sources by considering monetary media sources, industry reports, well-qualified conclusions, and online discussions. This can assist you with acquiring a balanced perspective available.

2. Utilize crucial investigation: Basic examination includes assessing fiscal summaries, organization execution, and market patterns to decide the inherent worth of a resource. This methodology assists you with evaluating the monetary wellbeing and possibilities of an organization prior to pursuing speculation choices.

3. specialized examination: Specialized investigation includes concentrating on value outlines, examples, and pointers to distinguish potential market patterns and make forecasts. This procedure is famous among momentary brokers and can supplement major examination.

4. Look for master counsel: Talking with monetary consultants or specialists can give important bits of knowledge and direction. Their insight and experience can assist you with exploring complex monetary choices and stay away from normal traps.

5. Use innovation instruments: Embrace innovation devices, for example, monetary applications, online stages, and investigation programming. These apparatuses can smooth out the social occasion and investigation of monetary data, saving time and further developing exactness.

For instance, consider what is going on where you need to put resources into a specific organization's stock. Gathering monetary data about the organization can include concentrating on its yearly reports, profit deliveries, and industry patterns. using essential examination, you can assess the organization's monetary proportions, development possibilities, and serious situation on the lookout. Moreover, consolidating specialized examination can assist with distinguishing likely passage and leave focuses in view of value examples and markers.

The Job of Chance Administration in Informed Direction

Informed dynamic in finance is firmly connected to viable gamble the board. Understanding and overseeing risk is fundamental to safeguard speculations and accomplish long haul monetary objectives. Here are a few critical standards of hazard the board:

1. Distinguish and survey gambles: The most important phase in risk the board is to recognize and evaluate the dangers related with a monetary choice. This includes dissecting likely dangers and their possible effect on your portfolio or speculation.

2. Broadening: Enhancing your portfolio is a deeply grounded risk the board methodology. By spreading your speculations across various resource classes and areas, you can relieve the effect of any single venture on your general portfolio.

3. Risk resistance: Decide your gamble resilience and adjust it to your venture procedure. This will assist you with pursuing choices that are in accordance with your solace level and long haul objectives.

4. Stop-misfortune orders: Use stop-misfortune orders to restrict possible misfortunes on ventures. A stop-misfortune request is a guidance to sell a resource on the off chance that its cost falls under a foreordained level. This system can assist with safeguarding your portfolio from huge misfortunes in unpredictable business sectors.

5. Risk-reward evaluation: Survey the possible dangers and compensations of a monetary choice. Consider the expected potential gain in contrast to the disadvantage chance and go with choices that offer a great gamble reward tradeoff.

For instance, envision you are thinking about putting resources into a high-development innovation stock. While the potential prizes might be alluring, the gamble of putting resources into an unstable area ought not be overlooked. Applying risk the executives standards, you could enhance your portfolio by likewise putting resources into stable, profit paying stocks to adjust the expected gamble of the innovation stock.

The Force of Innovation in Monetary Navigation

Innovation has reformed dynamic in the monetary business. It has empowered quicker and more exact information examination, further developed correspondence and cooperation, and opened up new roads for venture. Here are a few different ways innovation has influenced monetary independent direction:

1. Robotization: The mechanization of routine undertakings possesses opened up energy for monetary experts to zero in on additional mind boggling navigation. computerized exchanging frameworks, robo-consultants, and monetary arranging programming have become instrumental in smoothing out venture processes.

2. enormous information examination: Innovation has empowered the assortment, stockpiling, and investigation of tremendous measures of information. Enormous information examination takes into account the recognizable proof of examples and patterns that might have recently slipped through the cracks. Monetary establishments can now use this innovation to acquire significant bits of knowledge into client conduct and market elements.

3. web based exchanging stages: Internet exchanging stages have made it simpler for people to get to monetary business sectors and settle on speculation choices. These stages give continuous market information, research devices, and the capacity to execute exchanges with a couple of snaps.

4. Portable applications: The ascent of versatile applications has settled on monetary choice making more open and advantageous. Financial backers can now screen their portfolio, place exchanges, and access monetary news and examination from the center of their hand.

An illustration of the force of innovation in monetary navigation should be visible in the ascent of robo-counselors. These computerized financial planning stages use calculations to oversee speculation portfolios in light of foreordained rules and chance resistances. By utilizing innovation, robo-counselors give financially savvy and proficient speculation answers for a large number of financial backers.

How to Remain Informed about Market Patterns and Monetary Occasions?

remaining informed about market patterns and monetary occasions is critical for settling on informed monetary choices. Here are a few techniques to keep yourself refreshed:

1. Follow monetary media sources: Routinely follow legitimate monetary media sources to keep yourself informed about the most recent market patterns, financial pointers, and industry improvements. News sources like Bloomberg, CNBC, and Monetary Times are known for giving convenient and precise monetary news.

2. Join proficient organizations: Join proficient organizations and affiliations connected with your field of interest. These organizations frequently coordinate meetings, courses, and online classes that give bits of knowledge from industry specialists and thought pioneers.

3. influence web-based entertainment: Follow industry experts, examiners, and monetary organizations via online entertainment stages like Twitter and LinkedIn. Numerous monetary specialists share significant bits of knowledge and investigation on these stages.

4. Monetary schedules: Use financial schedules to follow impending financial occasions and information discharges. Financial schedules give data on key pointers, for example, loan cost choices, Gross domestic product development, and work information. These pointers can altogether affect monetary business sectors.

5. Utilize monetary bulletins and examination reports: Buy into monetary pamphlets and exploration reports from legitimate sources. These distributions frequently give top to bottom examination and suggestions on different speculation potential open doors.

For instance, envision you are keen on putting resources into the innovation area. By following significant monetary media sources, going to industry meetings, and drawing in with experts via web-based entertainment, you can acquire bits of knowledge into the most recent patterns, arising advances, and potential speculation amazing open doors inside the area.

The Significance of Enhancement in Monetary Portfolios

Broadening is a basic guideline of sound monetary navigation. It includes spreading your speculations across various resources, areas, or geographic districts to diminish the gamble of misfortune. Here are a few motivations behind why enhancement is significant:

1. Risk decrease: Enhancement assists with lessening the gamble of misfortune related with individual ventures. By spreading your ventures, you limit your openness to the exhibition of any single resource or market.

2. Smoother returns: Broadening can prompt smoother speculation returns over the long haul. By enhancing your portfolio, you can counterbalance misfortunes from failing to meet expectations resources with gains from different resources. This can assist with safeguarding your portfolio during market slumps.

3. Openness to various open doors: Expansion permits you to access and profit from various venture open doors. By putting resources into different resource classes and areas, you are bound to partake in the development of various enterprises and economies.

4. Rebalancing potential: Expansion offers the open door to rebalance your portfolio occasionally. Rebalancing includes changing your resource allotment to align it back with your ideal gamble bring profile back. This guarantees that your portfolio stays lined up with your drawn out objectives.

An illustration of the significance of enhancement should be visible in the 2008 worldwide monetary emergency. Numerous financial backers who had vigorously gathered their portfolios in a solitary resource class, like land, experienced huge misfortunes. The people who had broadened across various resource classes, like stocks, bonds, and items, fared better during the emergency.

Ways to further develop Your Monetary Critical thinking abilities

successful monetary critical thinking abilities can be created and worked on after some time. Here are a few hints to upgrade your critical thinking skills:

1. Ceaseless learning: Remain inquisitive and focused on constantly finding out about money and venture standards. Understand books, go to workshops, and take online courses to extend your insight and understanding.

2. Gain from previous slip-ups: Ponder past monetary choices and distinguish the mix-ups and examples learned. Utilize these encounters to illuminate future direction and try not to rehash comparative mistakes.

3. Look for different viewpoints: Abstain from falling into preference for non threatening information by searching out assorted viewpoints and assessments. Participate in conversations with specialists, talk with guides, and draw in with peers who have various perspectives.

4. Practice tolerance: Try not to pursue rushed choices in view of momentary market developments or feelings. Practice persistence and discipline by finding opportunity to examine and assess the accessible data completely.

5. Keep a drawn out viewpoint: center around the drawn out objectives and targets of your monetary choices. Try not to get influenced by transient market changes or commotion.

By integrating these tips into your dynamic interaction, you can foster the abilities and mentality important to settle on educated and effective monetary choices.

Informed dynamic in the monetary business sectors is urgent for accomplishing monetary objectives and moderating dangers. By figuring out the significance of data, evaluating key elements, using information investigation, and utilizing successful techniques, people and organizations can go with additional educated choices. Furthermore, perceiving the job of chance administration, utilizing the force of innovation, and remaining informed about market patterns are fundamental parts of informed direction. By reliably expanding portfolios and further developing monetary critical thinking abilities, financial backers can upgrade their odds of coming out on top in the dynamic and complex universe of money.

CHAPTER 5:

Advertising Authority for Business Achievement

Is it true that you are searching for the vital methodologies to assist your business with developing? Do you need an inside and out take a gander at the fundamental advances expected to guarantee a fruitful and flourishing business? Indeed, look no further!

This section gives 8 fundamental procedures to business development that will put you on the way towards making progress. We'll investigate creative strategies and counsel from experienced experts with the goal that you can partake in a smooth tasks process and growing client base. So on the off chance that you're prepared to turn into a relentless power of progress - we should begin!

Distinguish your objective market

In the event that you're beginning a business, recognizing your objective market is basic to your prosperity. You want to know who your client is, what they like, and how they like to purchase. When you have this data, you can fit your advertising approach and informing to all the more likely impact them.

For example, in the event that your objective market is a more established segment, conventional promoting techniques, like print advertisements and boards, might be more powerful. Be that as it may, assuming you are focusing on a more youthful crowd, virtual entertainment promoting can demonstrate more productive.

Realizing your objective market implies you're not squandering your assets attempting to contact individuals who aren't keen on the thing you're advertising. So find opportunity to do some statistical surveying and ensure you're contacting the ideal individuals with your items or administrations.

That, yet you can likewise utilize this exploration to illuminate your item improvement technique. By understanding who your clients are and what they need, you can make better items that meet their inclinations and requirements.

Foster a showcasing plan

Is it true that you are hoping to extend your business and arrive at additional expected clients? Fostering a promoting plan is urgent to draw in a more extensive crowd and develop your client base. You can plan your own bite the dust struck pins, use conventional showcasing techniques, or even run an online entertainment crusade. The initial step is to distinguish your objective segment and figure out their necessities and inclinations.

From that point, you can create a reasonable message and select the best channels to contact them. Whether it's through online entertainment promoting, email showcasing, or customary publicizing, having a clear cut plan can assist you with accomplishing your showcasing objectives and produce more deals. With the right technique set up, you can set your strategy in motion and begin contacting new clients in a matter of seconds.

Moreover, ensure you have examination set up to gauge the progress of your showcasing endeavors. Along these lines, you can follow what's working and make changes when required. Additionally, it's useful to have information available while introducing your outcomes to financial backers and different partners.

Improve your web-based presence

In the present computerized age, having major areas of strength for a presence is vital for organizations of any size. By putting resources into computerized showcasing systems, you can upgrade your perceivability and draw in additional clients. From website streamlining to virtual entertainment publicizing, there are different methods that can assist with expanding your internet based reach.

By utilizing these strategies, you can all the more likely associate with your interest group and drive more traffic to your site. So why pause? Begin putting resources into advanced showcasing today and take your web-based presence to a higher level. Likewise, remember to upgrade your site for cell phones, so you can arrive at clients in a hurry.

Remember that staying up with the latest is significant. This implies routinely refreshing your site and online entertainment channels with top notch content that is pertinent to your objective market. Additionally, you ought to keep steady over latest things in the business so you can stay serious and keep on drawing in clients.

Use virtual entertainment stages

Virtual entertainment stages assume a huge part in how organizations connect with their crowd. With a large number of dynamic clients on these stages, organizations can take advantage of a totally new client base that they might not have reached in any case. However, it's not just about the numbers. Virtual entertainment offers an exceptional chance to draw in with clients in a more private and bona fide manner.

Brands can make areas of strength for a presence by sharing significant substance, answering input, and connecting with their devotees. Thus, assuming you're hoping to expand your scope and draw in with your clients, now is the ideal time to begin using the force of online entertainment stages. Remember to think up a substance system ahead of time and ensure you have the fundamental assets set up.

Besides, you can use these stages to direct people to your site and lift brand mindfulness. Online entertainment is an extraordinary device for driving deals and transformations, so ensure you're making the most of its true capacity.

Increment client devotion programs

Clients are the backbone of any business. They are the ones who keep the money streaming and the deals expanding. Along these lines, it's vital for keep them blissful and locked in. One method for doing this is by offering devotion programs that give limits and motivations to bringing customers back. These projects increment client maintenance as well as assist with building brand devotion.

By showing clients that you esteem their business and will remunerate their steadfastness, you give a convincing motivation to them to make want more. Thus, this converts into expanded benefits and development for your business. Thus, on the off chance that you're not previously offering client unwaveringness programs, now is the ideal time to begin!

A speedy tip: Offer unwaveringness compensates that line up with your objective market's requirements and inclinations. Along these lines, you can guarantee that your program is alluring to them and propel them to make want more.

Center around higher expectations no matter what

In a world that appears to ceaselessly request more, the idea of zeroing in on higher expectations without ever compromising can some of the time be ignored. In any case, giving items or administrations of the greatest quality conceivable is a fundamental part of guaranteeing consumer loyalty and long haul achievement.

Quality draws in and holds clients, yet it likewise advances positive verbal exchange showcasing and can eventually prompt expanded benefits. It's critical to require the investment and work to guarantee that each part of the item or administration gave meets or surpasses assumptions.

In doing as such, organizations can construct a strong standing for conveying greatness and position themselves as pioneers in their industry. Hence, it's fundamental for organizations to focus on higher standards without compromise, as it is the way to long haul achievement and client unwaveringness.

Ensure your business is apparent

Regardless of how incredible your items or administrations are, on the off chance that potential clients can't find you, then, at that point, it won't make any difference. That is the reason it's crucial for ensure that your business is all around as apparent as conceivable to guarantee that individuals understand what you offer.

This could incorporate conventional techniques, for example, paper and radio promoting or more present day approaches like site improvement and pay-per-click crusades. It means quite a bit to zero in on nearby perceivability, as this can be exceptionally helpful for private ventures.

By utilizing strategies, for example, geo-designated publicizing or improving your site for neighborhood Website optimization, you can guarantee that possible clients in your space are bound to find you while looking on the web. Remember that perceivability is key for any business, so ensure you're putting resources into the right systems to get your name out there.

Remember your current clients

Zeroing in on getting new customers is simple. Nonetheless, it's memorable's essential that your current clients are similarly as significant and ought not be overlooked. Building solid associations with existing clients can assist with expanding client dependability and rehash business.

You can do this by consistently conveying bulletins, offering limits or unique offers, holding occasions, or just captivating with them via online entertainment. Zeroing in on your current clients can be an extraordinary method for showing your appreciation and make them want more and more.

Hence, assuming you believe your business should succeed, it's vital for center around drawing in new clients as well as supporting associations with existing ones. Not exclusively will this assist your business with developing, however it can likewise be a strong showcasing instrument.

Notwithstanding the systems framed above, there are numerous different strategies that organizations can use to build their scope and draw in clients. Notwithstanding, the main thing is to have an arrangement set up and guarantee that you are consistently putting time and assets into your computerized presence. This will assist with guaranteeing that your business stays serious and keeps on developing for quite a long time into the future.

Last contemplations

It is fundamental for organizations to stay cutthroat and draw in clients in the advanced age. Doing so requires an arrangement that includes utilizing virtual entertainment stages, making faithfulness programs, zeroing in on higher standards when in doubt, ensuring your business is noticeable on the web, and sustaining associations with existing clients.

With these methodologies set up, you can guarantee that your business stays cutthroat and keeps on developing. Keep in mind: the way to progress lies in understanding individuals' opinion on what you offer — and utilizing this information to think up a compelling advertising technique.

Remember that an effective business procedure is certainly not a mind-blowing phenomenon. It requires investment to assemble connections and gain entrust with clients, yet with devotion and the well thought out plan set up, you should rest assured that your business will arrive at its maximum capacity!

Successful Marking and Situating

Before you contribute the time, cash, and energy into fostering another brand, it's essential to ensure that your expected clients will remember it accordingly.

A brand situating procedure assists you with ensuring your image can be effortlessly recognized by its main interest group and recognizes it from different brands in the commercial center.

It's likewise an unquestionably helpful instrument while promoting your image to your expected crowd and guaranteeing that they know precisely exact thing esteem you give them. Here are the fundamental components of a fruitful brand situating technique.

Why is brand situating significant?

A brand situating methodology is significant for two reasons. To start with, it guarantees that you will actually want to hang out in a cutthroat commercial center. Second, it offers you the chance to present your image as something one of a kind and not quite the same as the opposition. A solid brand situating technique will assist with laying out your organization's character and the way things are seen by likely clients. The ultimate objective is to make an enduring impact on the customer so they will pick your business over another.

What's the significance here for my business?

It is essential to foster a powerful brand situating system to assist your business with sticking out. Without this technique, you are just speculating concerning what will turn out best for your business and what message you need to depict. Fostering a powerful brand situating procedure assists you with articulating the basic beliefs and key messages of your business that are generally significant and applicable to target clients.

What are the seven components?

A brand situating system is the groundwork of any effective brand. The seven fundamental components are: market class, interest group, USP, brand separation, brand character, brand personality and evaluating system. There's something else to it besides making a logo, naming your organization, and sorting out where you need to be in the commercial center. It requires investment and scrupulousness to characterize your identity as an association so that individuals can relate to your item or administration. It likewise expects imagination to foster a true voice that conveys what separates your organization from others in its field.

The brand position ought to be imparted reliably across all channels, including web-based entertainment stages. Recall that all correspondences should be lined up with the general message so they don't confound or occupy from the organization's image story.

1) Market Class

Concluding which market class, subcategory or making another class to situate a brand under is a significant choice. Market classes are not made equivalent, and designating assets to an essential market classification can be the distinction among progress and disappointment. So before you begin fostering your image situating methodology, ponder what kind of market classification you need to contend in. Ask yourself inquiries like:

• Who is my interest group?
• What do I have that no other person does?
• Who are my rivals? Also, what makes me not the same as them?
At times, where the market is profoundly packed or considered a red sea market (loads of organizations battling one another) it tends to

merit situating your image in a sub-classification or making a completely new classification (blue sea) for your situating procedure. this can diminish the quantity of contenders you need to go up against or eliminate any rivalry through and through. This is an incredible method for building an exceptional brand with an engaged interest group and novel incentive yet it accompanies a compromise, marks that make new classifications or go into less popular sub-classifications will likewise need to showcase and advance the class as well as the brand.

For instance the very first caffeinated drink needed to initially showcase what caffeinated drinks were and the advantages to the interest group close by appending their image to that class.

2) Interest group

A brand situating methodology characterizes your image and separates you from the opposition. Assuming done well, it will assist with developing your crowd and make them bound to purchase your item or administration. To do this, you'll have to know who your interest group is. Knowing the character attributes of your interest group will permit you to fit informing to their particular requirements and concerns. For instance, in the event that you're selling athletic shoes, showcasing to individuals who have a functioning way of life will be unique in relation to focusing on somebody who doesn't practice by any means.

Understanding your main interest group and the trouble spots, goals, fears and protests they have will assist you with making an engaged and designated brand situating and incentive to resound with this crowd. A critical piece of powerful brand situating is importance to your ideal interest group in the event that they are confounded by or don't comprehend your class or the job you play in their life they won't probably ever purchase from you and battle to recollect you. Compelling situating and brand memorability remain closely connected the better more right on track your situating system is the more opportunity of crowd acknowledgment and purchase in you'll have.

Past socioeconomics, your crowd's psychographics are vital to comprehend their thought process, feel, act and their shopper propensities, it is in these triggers, values and convictions that can assist you with making a situating ing technique that is significant and customized to their particular necessities, difficulties and wants.

3) Recognize your novel selling recommendation

What makes your business unique in relation to other people? This is the main inquiry you want to respond to while fostering your image situating system. Your USP, or Remarkable Selling Recommendation characterizes what separates your business from rivals and how you enhance the ideal interest group. USPs normally come to fruition in one of two ways:

1) through an item or administration benefit, like ensured fulfillment;

2) through how the item is situated in the commercial center, like The World's Best Apples.

To start to reveal your USP you can go through a course of posting all that makes you unique and trimming this down to 2 or 3 top choices that the opposition can't guarantee (so do your examination first). Then, at that point, ponder how you would showcase every one of these USP's the one that is more straightforward to expand upon, produce imaginative thoughts for and concoct promoting lobbies for is ordinarily the one to zero in on. Your interesting selling suggestion additionally needs to be basic and succinct so you don't confound your crowd or upset memorability.

Stay away from conventional Usp's, for instance, 'client support' this is the sort of thing your clients will expect and most of organizations discuss and except if you will go the lengths of Zappos and be the world's best at client assistance stay away from these effectively imitated suggestions. Marking is about intentional separation as a matter of some importance and furthermore constructing a faultless situation for your business on the off chance that you follow every other person you disrupt both of these norms.

4) Brand Separation

Separation is a significant piece of any situating technique and can take many structures. Whether you need to separate your image based on cost, quality, brand insight, item plan, visual character, character or something completely different, separation is vital to guaranteeing that your image stands apart from the opposition. To foster a fruitful promoting procedure, it's essential to comprehend what separates you from different brands in a similar space and to twofold down on this in your missions, natural showcasing and through your group consistently. As said above marking is about conscious separation and you can do this across each region in your business from the plan of action as Dollar Shave Club did in the razor market with a membership model or through working on an industry through creative item configuration like Apple did.

The more ways you can separate the better and particularly need to use your own image character and visual personality. A great deal of organizations duplicate the opposition in the manner they market, how they market and how they introduce themselves and at times you have entire businesses by which you can't differentiate between the organizations in them, these stale business sectors are prepared for disturbance and change.

5) Brand Character

Brand character is a significant piece of your image situating system. It can assume an instrumental part in speaking with your clients, and it recognizes you from contenders. By adjusting your image to a character, you'll have the option to more readily distinguish who ought to be focused on as the end client (i.e., top of the line versus frugal), which thus will assist you with making more designated showcasing messages. When you grasp your main interest group and have made your incentive and separation technique you'll be better positioned to foster your image's character and quite possibly of the most effective way to do this is to utilize brand models to make an original blend novel to you that can recognize you from the opposition.

Models are unmistakable person characters that have been in need for large number of purpose in stories, folklore and from the beginning of time. They are additionally jobs we take all through our lives relying upon specific circumstances and we likewise search for individuals to fill these jobs in our day to day existence at various times we are permanently set up to perceive these characters and search them out at various times. Every paradigm is lined up with a client need or want so In the event that you know your interest group is feeling at the point not long prior to collaborating with your image you can fabricate your image's character type on the model they are looking for.

An illustration of this is a money manager who is moderately aged and works for an enormous monetary establishment in the city, they go to work ordinary same daily schedule to a similar office, in a huge dark structure to a little work space and do this process again consistently. It doesn't take a lot to understand that he may be needing opportunity, resistance and the open street, this cautions his psyche to pay special attention to or look for brands, valuable open doors and life altering situations lined up with defiance, opportunity and possibly at the outrageous disorder. To this end a brand like Harley Davidson leaps out at him right now in his life and Harley Davidson imparts the soul of the Criminal Paradigm by displaying pictures of open streets and non-similarity. They additionally blend the fugitive in with the Adventurer using images of wings and the Everyperson inclining toward the soul of local area.

Assuming you make a clear cut brand character it can tune a dull tasteless brand into a significant, attractive contribution for your crowd that whenever done accurately will attract your optimal crowd to you.

6) Brand Personality

What does your image personality say regarding your image? Your image personality can be anything from the organization's name, to its logo, to the tone wherein it speaks with clients. The job that your image personality plays in your situating technique relies upon what you believe individuals should be familiar with your item or administration. To do this, you should initially settle on the kind of situating system you might want to utilize and afterward pick a character that best suits it. Your marking ought to match your situating methodology on the grounds that an unfortunate match will prompt disarray among purchasers and even reason them to connect themselves with the brand adversely. Your image character is comprised of four layers:

Center (Heart of the brand) - The establishment for a successful brand personality incorporates reason, vision, mission and values

System (Mind of the brand) - The essential viewpoint to your image incorporates situating and separation

Correspondence (Character of the brand) - The manner in which you impart to your crowd incorporates character, manner of speaking, informing and showcasing

Configuration (Face of the brand) - The visual viewpoint to your image incorporates logo, colors, textual styles, insurance, signage, item configuration, bundling

To actually situate your image these four layers should be brought together and in complete arrangement.

7) Cost

Your evaluating methodology will assume a significant part in your image situating technique, particularly in the event that you're offering to buyers. It's vital to consider what position you believe your image should accept on the lookout and what cutthroat estimating will mean for that position. For instance, on the off chance that you maintain that your image should be viewed as reasonable and available, having low costs is critical. In any case, if you need to offer top of the line extravagance merchandise for a selective customer base then greater costs are more proper. You ought to likewise contemplate cost according to the viewpoint of client brain research. Certain individuals partner lower costs with incredible worth while others partner greater costs with quality items. To sort out which approach is best for your image, it should direct research on who your objective client base is and what they understand to be true with regards to evaluating related subjects like worth and cost adequacy.

A brand situating system is significant for any business, paying little heed to measure or industry. The way to situating your image for progress is having a technique that is custom-made to your extraordinary business and circumstance.

Our aide has assisted you with managing the seven fundamental components expected to create your own effective situating technique. Presently it is the ideal time to begin executing what you've realized!

Associating with Your Interest group

Knowing how to arrive at your objective market is the best way to build your portion of the overall industry and further develop deals. Miss the point entirely, and your funds might endure.

Anyway, how might you arrive at your interest group and get them inspired by your item or administration?

What is an ideal interest group?

A main interest group is a particular gathering of shoppers distinguished by you as probably going to need your item or administration. They are purchasers you trust will ultimately turn into your clients. Interest groups can be directed by age, orientation, area, pay, interests, or other segment data, for example, their work titles or those with a specific trouble spot or at a specific life stage.

Why knowing how to arrive at your interest group is significant

It's useful to know who your ideal interest group is. Yet, in the event that you don't have the foggiest idea how to contact them, you'll battle to get your image and items before them.

Knowing how to arrive at your ideal interest group is significant on the grounds that:

- It assists you with advertising more brilliant: Having understanding into what works and what doesn't can assist you with putting resources into compelling efforts and pull back on the duds.

- It impacts item improvement: Characterizing the obstacles and desires different interest groups face can help you plan and test items that are pertinent and appealing.

- It increments income: Designated advertising allows you to zero in on the endeavors and crowd portions that produce the most ridiculously income — or, then again, allows you to dissect why different sections aren't changing over.

Step by step instructions to arrive at your interest group: 8 compelling systems

Prepared to arrive at your ideal interest group? Here are moves toward begin.

1. Characterize your interest group

2. Realize where your crowd is dynamic

3. Make pertinent substance

4. Utilize designated promoting

5. Work with powerhouses

6. Make a reference program

7. Use hashtags via virtual entertainment

8. Keep in contact with your crowd

1. Characterize your ideal interest group

To begin with, you want to realize who you're focusing before you can contact them. Characterize your interest groups:

- Have a strong comprehension of your items and who could profit from them

- Take a gander at your current client profiles and do crowd research

- Go further than segment data and investigate psychographic information

- Make center interest group fragments

- Look at your rivals and their client base

Understanding who your interest group is educates each and every other part regarding your advertising procedure.

2. Realize where your crowd is dynamic

After you distinguish your ideal interest group, now is the right time to sort out where they hang out on the web and how they like to interface with brands. Do they invest a large portion of their energy on Instagram? Do they incline toward exchange distributions over corporate online journals? Understanding where your interest group is generally dynamic on the web (and disconnected) will assist you with conveying your message on the right stages.

3. Make applicable substance

Your substance is the message you're shipping off your main interest group. Attempt to grasp their special necessities and battles and make content that responds to them. Consider making blog entries, email bulletins, online entertainment content, promotions, recordings, or other substance to partake in pertinent networks and use information to make a greater amount of the stuff your interest group loves.

4. Utilize designated promoting

"Make and they will come" isn't generally evident, particularly for new shippers.

Utilize designated promotion missions to contact your crowd on the stages they're dynamic on. Google advertisements and virtual entertainment promotions generally offer high level focusing on abilities to assist you with contacting individuals who matter. You can focus on your missions in light of different attributes and ways of behaving of your crowd, including their age, area, online interests, life stage, work job, and pay. This guarantees your promotions are simply displayed to individuals who will more probable be keen on your image and items.

5. Work with powerhouses

Powerhouse promoting includes working with individuals who've fabricated notorieties around a particular specialty, and a local area that takes care of that specialty. Powerhouses make content for their channels, advance your image, and, consequently, assist you with making more deals. Collaborate with powerhouses whose crowds are loaded with individuals you might want to reach, make content that shows your image in its best light, and utilize the powerhouse's pre-fabricated trust to drive their crowd to your own site and stages.

6. Make a reference program

Reference programs urge your current clients to prescribe your items to their loved ones — a.k.a. individuals who are probably going to be comparable in needs, necessities, and qualities.

An old yet significant Nielson concentrate on shows that suggestions from loved ones are the most solid type of publicizing, and boosting blissful clients with cash back, future limits, and free items is an incredible method for encouraging nearer associations with your

7. Use hashtags via virtual entertainment

The right hashtags via web-based entertainment channels like Instagram and TikTok can expand your scope and draw in your main interest group. Find hashtags that are moving in your specialty and integrate them into posts on your web-based entertainment channels. This will guarantee you appear in the feeds of individuals who are effectively looking for that hashtag and important substance.

8. Keep in contact with your crowd

At the point when you've figured out how to arrive at your objective clients, the last thing you maintain that should do is leave them hanging or vanish totally. Keep in contact with individuals you arrive at by empowering them to pursue your email list, sending customary, significant messages, and proceeding to associate with them on their number one web-based entertainment stages.

Step by step instructions to arrive at your main interest group for an independent company

Characterizing and arriving at your ideal interest group is basic to the outcome of your independent company. At the point when you comprehend who you're focusing on, what stages your crowd is generally dynamic on, and the kind of satisfied they need, advancing your image and sell your products is a lot simpler.

Stand apart from the opposition by supporting associations with your interest group. This is a recap of the way you can do that:

1. Characterize who your main interest group is and where they invest their energy.

2. Make applicable substance for your interest group in light of their novel needs and needs.

3. Pick the channels you'll zero in on to arrive at your main interest group and use stage explicit strategies to expand your perceivability.

4. Run powerhouse showcasing efforts to grow your scope.

5. Make a reference program to urge existing clients to impart your items to their loved ones.

6. Remember about your current clients! Keep in contact to cultivate further associations with individuals who as of now purchase from you.

Step by step instructions to arrive at your interest group: Important points

It's a lot more straightforward to sell your items and become your web based business store while you're focusing on the ideal individuals on the channels they like. The more information you get on your current clients, the more you can focus on specialty crowd sections to guarantee you're conveying profoundly applicable substance on the best stages.

At the point when you're simply getting everything rolling, ensure you have a characterized interest group. Then, at that point, sort out where that crowd invests their energy, make pertinent substance, and use strategies like collaborating with powerhouses, consolidating hashtags, and reference projects to assist you with contacting them.

Instructions to arrive at your ideal interest group FAQ

How would you arrive at an ideal interest group in promoting?

- Characterize who your interest group is and where they invest their energy.
- Make applicable substance that addresses their requirements.
- Utilize designated promoting to contact the perfect individuals.
- Collaborate with powerhouses to build your perceivability.
- Make a reference program to exploit individual suggestions.
- Use hashtags in your web-based entertainment posts.
- Remember about your current clients!

What are 5 things you should consider for your main interest group?

1. Segment data like their age, orientation, and area.
2. Psychographic information, similar to their difficulties, interests, and yearnings.

3. The stages they continuous the most.

4. What content they need and need from you.

5. How you'll make a continuous relationship with them.

What are the 3 objective market methodologies?

1. Separated promoting: When a brand makes individual lobbies for a few different interest groups or fragments.

2. Concentrated promoting: When a brand makes one showcasing message for a solitary, specialty interest group.

3. Undifferentiated showcasing: When a brand makes one mission with similar directive for its whole crowd.

CHAPTER 6:

Legitimate Shields: Safeguarding Your Riches

Creating financial momentum takes time and exertion, and it is fundamental to safeguard it from potential dangers that can think twice about monetary security. Resource assurance is the method involved with protecting your abundance from claims, leasers, or other monetary dangers that could hurt your monetary strength. Executing resource assurance procedures can assist with moderating dangers and safeguard your resources. Here are successful resource assurance systems for shielding your riches:

Laying out a Trust

A trust is a legitimate element made to oversee and safeguard resources. Trusts can be utilized for various purposes, including keeping away from probate, diminishing assessments, and safeguarding resources from claims and lender claims. By moving resources for a trust, people can restrict their obligation and shield their resources from likely lawful activity. There are various kinds of trusts accessible, including revocable trusts, permanent trusts, and resource security trusts. It is fundamental to talk with an accomplished domain arranging lawyer to figure out which sort of trust is the most appropriate for your singular necessities.

Making a Restricted Responsibility Organization (LLC)

In the event that you are an entrepreneur, making a different lawful substance, for example, a restricted risk organization (LLC) or partnership, can give security to your own resources against potential business liabilities. By isolating your own resources from your business resources, you can limit your openness to legitimate dangers and safeguard your privately invested money in case of a claim or other business-related chances.

Buying Protection

Protection is one of the best ways of safeguarding your resources. Various sorts of insurance contracts, like extra security, health care coverage, property holder's protection, and collision protection, give monetary assurance against startling occasions that could cause monetary misfortune. It is fundamental to assess your protection inclusion consistently to guarantee it lines up with your ongoing monetary circumstance. Also, you, with the help of your Bequest Arranging Lawyer, could frame an Irreversible Extra security Trust (ILIT); call us to figure out more.

Setting up Retirement Records

Retirement accounts, for example, 401(k)s and IRAs, give critical resource insurance against claims and banks. By and large, these records are safeguarded under government liquidation regulation, and that implies they can't be seized by leasers or used to fulfill decisions. By putting resources into retirement accounts, you can construct a significant savings while likewise defending your abundance against possible dangers.

Resource Naming

Resource naming is the course of legitimately moving responsibility for to shield them from likely loan bosses or claims. By moving resources for a trust, you can give an additional layer of insurance against likely monetary dangers. It is fundamental for work with an educated lawyer or monetary counselor to guarantee that resource naming is done accurately and lawfully.

Giving

Giving resources for relatives or trusts can be a compelling resource insurance system. By moving resources for a trust, people can eliminate resources from their domain and safeguard them from expected banks.

Resource assurance is pivotal for people who have attempted to amass riches. By utilizing the systems framed above, people can shield their heritage from likely legitimate activity, claims, and lender claims. Nevada is ostensibly the best State to get this degree of assurance.

Broaden Your Speculation Portfolio: Enhancement is a basic technique for overseeing risk and safeguarding your riches. By spreading your speculations across different resource classes, enterprises, and geographic districts, you can lessen the effect of market variances and limit likely misfortunes.

Consistently survey and change your venture portfolio to guarantee it stays lined up with your gamble resilience, monetary objectives, and economic situations. Talk with a monetary guide to assist you with fostering a broadened speculation system custom-made to your particular requirements and targets.

Lay out a Backup stash: A just-in-case account fills in as a monetary wellbeing net, giving a pad to startling costs or pay disturbances. Plan to save three to a half year of everyday costs in a promptly open, okay record, for example, a high return bank account or currency market reserve.

Having a rainy day account set up can assist you with abstaining from taking advantage of your ventures or bringing about exorbitant premium obligation during testing monetary times, eventually shielding your drawn out riches.

Execute Resource Insurance Methodologies: Resource security systems can assist with protecting your abundance from likely dangers, like claims, liquidation, or lender claims. Contingent upon your particular circumstance, you might consider techniques like setting up trusts, laying out a restricted obligation organization (LLC), or getting proper protection inclusion.

Talk with a lawyer or monetary organizer to decide the most reasonable resource insurance systems for your conditions and guarantee they are executed accurately.

Survey and Update Your Domain Plan: An exhaustive bequest plan is fundamental for guaranteeing that your abundance is circulated by your desires and in the most potential duty effective way. Consistently audit and update your home intend to represent changes in your monetary circumstance, individual connections, or assessment regulations.

Work with a domain arranging lawyer to make or refresh your will, lay out trusts, assign recipients, and execute other home arranging apparatuses that line up with your objectives and protect your abundance for people in the future.

Safeguarding your abundance requires a proactive and vital way to deal with overseeing chances, broadening ventures, and carrying out fitting shields. By following these fundamental tips, you can get your monetary future and guarantee that your well deserved resources proceed to develop and serve your requirements all through your lifetime and then some.

Lawful Fundamentals for Entrepreneurs

Beginning an independent company includes a few lawful advances. Following lawful necessities is essential to guarantee your business stays consistent and productive. As an entrepreneur, it ultimately depends on you to explore relevant regulations and follow them. This cycle can be overwhelming from the get go, so I've assembled an agenda of essential legitimate prerequisites you'll need to survey prior to beginning your independent venture.

10 Legitimate Prerequisites for Beginning an Independent company

I. Pick a Business Construction

A business structure is a legitimate construction that decides significant parts of your business, for example, how you make good on charges, if and how you are permitted to raise capital, who possesses the organization, and how benefits are disseminated. While thinking about which

business design to pick, begin by posing yourself
a couple of inquiries:

- What are my short-and long haul business
  objectives?

- What sort of administrations am I giving?

- Do I intend to enlist workers later on, or
  will this be an independent undertaking?

- What capital do I have accessible and
  what future monetary necessities do I
  have?

Gathering this data will assist with illuminating
your decision. Each individual has various
requirements for their business, and lawful
elements are not a one-size-fits-all arrangement.
While certain people might feel their work
conveys little gamble of legitimate activity,
others might decide to situate their organization
for greater development that could convey more
gamble.

Four business structure choices to consider while beginning a private venture:

1. Sole Owner

Numerous free movers start their process as sole owners. For charge purposes, sole owners by and large work under their own Government backed retirement number, however you can apply for a Citizen Recognizable proof Number (TIN) for your business all things being equal. This business structure requires negligible administrative work and offers adaptability assuming that you choose to independent parttime.

2. Restricted Risk Organization (LLC)

A LLC (Restricted Risk Organization) is a business structure that gives a center ground between working a company and a sole ownership: it considers the pass-through tax collection from a sole ownership while likewise giving the restricted responsibility of an enterprise. LLCs are famous because of their straightforwardness, while giving solid legitimate securities of a company that safeguard individual resources. Consider it the subsequent stage over a sole ownership.

3. S Partnership

With a S Partnership, or S-Corp, benefits and misfortunes go through to the investor's very own expense form, so the actual business isn't burdened. The investor should be paid an honest evaluation, however any extra benefit isn't dependent upon independent work charge.

4. C Enterprise

With a C Enterprise, or C-Corp, you are the larger part investor of your organization. This business structure gives restricted responsibility, isolating your own and proficient resources. While this construction is one of the most complicated business game plans accessible, it is additionally the most modern, making it an appealing choice for free thinkers.

II. Register Your Business Name

In the event that you decide to maintain your business as a Sole Owner, the name of the business will default to the name of the proprietor's lawful name. For instance, in the event that you go by Rachel Smith and you structure a counseling organization, the lawful name of the business will be "Rachel Smith." Notwithstanding, in the event that you choose to name your organization "Rachel Smith Counseling," you'll have to enlist this as a DBA name.

This cycle tells your state or nearby government the name you are working your business under. This permits you to make and utilize the name you need for marking without integrating. Explicit DBA enlistment rules shift from one state to another.

For the individuals who are recording a lawful element, an application should be documented with your state for either Articles of Joining or Articles of Association. Whether you pick a LLC, S Corp, or C-Corp in sync one above, you should document a name for the organization with your state.

III. Brand Names, Logos, or Trademarks

Assuming you are anticipating working broadly or offering on the web types of assistance, you might need to consider getting your business name reserved. A DBA name or consolidated business name won't offer brand security in the 49 states where your business isn't enrolled. While reserving isn't a necessity, it will give more grounded security to your image. This interaction includes applying for a brand name with the U.S. Patent and Brand name Office. If you would like to seek after a brand name, begin by directing a thorough inquiry to ensure the name you need to utilize is accessible.

9 Methods for building an Individual Brand for Independent company

Building an individual brand is a significant piece of your personality — whether you're a free proficient or a Fortune 100 organization.

From your name and logo to your organization motto and notoriety, it's the means by which the public knows you.

As a self employed entity, you are the essence of your organization. Laying out serious areas of strength for a brand is vital for the development and progress of your business.

The following are nine methods for building an individual brand.

1. Lay out Acknowledgment: Consider what separates you. A few brands are immediately conspicuous, even without words. Buyers all over the planet perceive Nike's universal "swoosh" logo or the notable brilliant curves of Mcdonald's. These brands, notwithstanding, address interesting special cases — even Starbucks confronted analysis over a logo change that eliminated their name.

The way to viable marking, for most organizations, starts with straightforwardly telling individuals your name. At the point when contacts or potential clients can rapidly lay out what your identity is, you've ventured out in fostering an association.

2. Give Data: Obviously make sense of what you do. Potential clients ought to never need to look for the fundamental data that characterizes your organization or business objectives. A few free experts address this by laying out a legitimate business name, for example, "John Smith's IT Counseling," however whether you utilize a business name or your own, your general marking ought to mirror a message that advances and lines up with your area of concentration.

3. Be Exceptional: Typify what separates you

While brand mindfulness is a fundamental initial step of building an individual brand, to be really effective, your marking ought to make the message a stride further. Exhibit the worth or advantages you offer that put you aside from your opposition. Offer imaginative strategies, an exceptional specialization, or industry-driving skill.

4. Be Paramount: Specialty an effective message

Your own image ought to make a significant message that assists you with standing apart from the group — for the right reasons. Beyond preposterous marking that incorporates contrivances or tricks might be powerful in assisting individuals with recollecting that you, however it can come at the expense of your expert standing.

5. Remain Predictable: Make visual coherence

All your marking endeavors — whether part of systems administration, promoting, or whatever other region that increments perceivability — ought to communicate a reliable subject and message. Visual parts, plan components, key data, and particularly by and large informing shouldn't fluctuate starting with one spot then onto the next.

6. Stay away from Disarray: Keep similar message across channels

As an autonomous expert, you are frequently seen as addressing your own image — even in your own life and activities. Remember this in your public, non-business correspondences and activities, including online entertainment organizations. Varying messages advanced by your own and proficient activities could make an impression of untrustworthiness or absence of reliability.

7. Let the news out: Make an internet based presence

A deeply grounded individual brand likewise needs a deeply grounded web-based presence in virtual entertainment, yet additionally on an expert site. A site is the ideal spot to feature your image and market your abilities.

8. Think about the 10,000 foot view: Construct a standing, in addition to a name

Giving your business card out to everybody you meet or publicizing in each exchange distribution you can find might assist individuals with learning your name, yet without a standing, establishing a genuine connection can be troublesome. That is the reason it's critical to make laying out skill and worth a center piece of your own marking message. Here are far to move toward this:

- Utilizing an unmistakable variety subject all through your visual marking, remembering for business cards, on your site, and as a component of your logo

- Inventive advertising endeavors, like the creative utilization of virtual entertainment

- Integrating a subject matter into your marking message

9. Assemble Believability: Spread the news about your business

Utilizing on the web outlets to share important industry data that teaches or illuminates others can assist with situating you as a specialist in your field and construct individual brand validity. This should be possible by laying out an organization blog, sharing data via virtual entertainment organizations, or effectively helping through discussions. Propose to talk at systems administration occasions or gatherings, or host your own, and energize informal exchange advancement by mentioning references from clients with whom you have laid areas of strength for out.

IV. Get a Business Distinguishing proof Number (EIN) from the IRS

Any business that works as a company or organization or has representatives will be expected to have a Business Recognizable proof Number (EIN) from the IRS. An EIN distinguishes your business for charge purposes — consider it a Government backed retirement number for your business — and you can use to start a business financial balance, record government forms, and apply for permits to operate.

The simplest method for applying for an EIN is online through the IRS EIN Colleague. On the off chance that you work as a sole ownership or single part LLC, you are not expected to get an EIN, in spite of the fact that getting one is a method for making extra division among business and individual responsibility and it will safeguard your government managed retirement number on business records and help safeguard against fraud.

V. Find out About State and Neighborhood Expenses

Personal expense is logical by all accounts not the only duty you are liable for paying into, so it's essential to comprehend other assessment necessities you might have. Most of self employed entities are viewed as independently employed and are along these lines subject to paying Independent work (SE) Duty notwithstanding personal expense. SE Assessment is both the business and worker parts of Government managed retirement and Federal health care (FICA).

Notwithstanding, there are conditions in which your duty circumstance might vary. For instance, what your business is organized may mean for which charges you are expected to pay into. What's more, whether your business created a critical gain during the previous year could likewise be an element.

VI. Get Required Licenses to operate and Licenses

Very much like some other business, self employed entities should get appropriate allows and licenses. Contingent upon your industry and where your business is found, you might should be authorized on the government level as well as on the state or neighborhood level. Government licenses are expected for organizations engaged with any kind of action that is directed and managed by a bureaucratic organization. State permitting and allows will fluctuate contingent upon area.

VII. Make a Consistence Plan

Indeed, even as an entrepreneur, you're dependent upon a portion of the regulations and guidelines that apply to huge organizations. These incorporate promoting, showcasing, finance, protected innovation, and security regulations. For organizations that have representatives, there are extra state and government guidelines that might should be kept situationally. The SBA has accommodating guidance for keeping your private company consistent.

Furthermore, private companies should guarantee that they are without a care in the world regarding project worker misclassification concerns. In addition to the fact that this is a danger to your business itself, yet in addition your future clients.

VIII. Open a Business Ledger

Legitimately, having a different ledger for deals will empower you to all the more likely track and report on your pay and costs. It is prudent to set up a business ledger before you begin getting installments from clients however it's shockingly better in the event that you do so when you fire setting up your business. Do all necessary investigation and track down a bank that best meets your requirements. You will frequently require a few snippets of data while starting a business financial balance, for example,

- Your EIN (Boss Distinguishing proof Number) or your government backed retirement number in the event that your business is a sole ownership

- Arrangement archives for your business

- Your possession understanding reports

- Your Permit to operate

IX. Acquire Business Protection

The choice to begin a private venture implies that you are liable for guaranteeing the lawful and monetary prosperity of your organization. Recall that you are your business — assuming any lawful or monetary issues emerge that influence your organization, they will likewise influence you straightforwardly. It's critical to safeguard your business against the gamble of obligation misfortunes not on the grounds that numerous clients will expect you to have these protections, however it additionally to safeguard yourself and your future security.

Obviously, the sorts of protection that are appropriate for your business will shift significantly and rely upon your industry, the size of your business, and the kind of clients you work with, among different elements. The following are a couple of normal sorts of business protection that numerous self employed entities convey:

1. General Risk Protection

General risk protection is many times fundamental for free thinkers. This protection covers a large number of occurrences, including unplanned harm to a client's property, cases of defamation or criticism, and the expense of guarding claims.

2. Blunders and Oversights Protection

Blunders and oversights protection, otherwise called proficient obligation protection, gives security in the occurrence that a client causes monetary mischief because of a mistake or exclusion — that is, a disappointment for your benefit to play out a vital piece of your obligation on a task.

3. Locally established Business Protection

While an insurance contract for a locally established business doesn't make a difference to everybody, it's important for free movers who decide to sort out of a work space. Most mortgage holders' insurance strategies don't cover misfortunes supported out of a work space, yet a protection contract for a locally situated business can give the security you and your clients need.

X. Consider How You Will Deal with Your Administrative center

Administrative center administration comprises of all of the regulatory and support assignments that should be finished to maintain your business. This incorporates recording administrative work, following costs, documenting assessments, and charging clients. While dealing with your administrative center isn't in fact a legitimate prerequisite, how you decide to deal with these errands can have lawful ramifications not too far off.

A few free thinkers decide to enlist regulatory help while others go the DIY course utilizing on the web instruments and tech to create solicitations, track costs, and bill clients. Others will utilize an expert help like MBO Benefit for help. Making arrangements for how you will deal with these obligations is a brilliant move as another entrepreneur and will permit you to zero in your time and consideration on clients as opposed to routine business upkeep.

Exploring Agreements and Arrangements

Beginning another business includes going into numerous significant legitimate agreements and arrangements. For business people without lawful foundations, the complex legitimate language can rapidly get overpowering.

This thorough aide analyzes key arrangements business people consistently experience, with basic clarifications of each agreement's motivation, basic statements, traps to keep away from, and ways to arrange positive terms.

With a superior comprehension of these essential business contracts, business visionaries can safeguard their inclinations and unhesitatingly deal with the lawful side of building an organization.

Normal Startup Agreements and Arrangements

Here are key sorts of agreements frequently utilized by business visionaries during the startup interaction:

Association Arrangements — Diagrams freedoms as well as certain limitations between business fellow benefactors. Subtleties proprietorship stakes, dynamic power, accomplice jobs, vesting periods, and so forth.

Investor Arrangements — Oversees relations between investors in the event that the business is set up as a partnership. Like organization arrangements.

Working Arrangements — Characterizes possession rates and working standards for restricted risk organizations (LLCs).

Speculation Arrangements — Illuminates the provisions of any venture adjusts, including financial backer freedoms.

Convertible Note Arrangements — Momentary obligation that believers into value partakes in future subsidizing adjusts. A startup supporting choice.

Credit Arrangements — Required in the event that acquiring bank funding or obligation. Subtleties reimbursement terms, interest, guarantee, and so forth.

Protected innovation Arrangements — Covers authorizing, eminences, secrecy, and responsibility for like licenses, brand names, and copyrights.

Association Arrangements

Association arrangements are fundamental for characterizing prime supporter privileges and staying away from future struggle. Key areas might cover:

— Determine each accomplice's proportionate possession stake. Considers vesting over the long haul.

Benefit/Misfortune Dissemination — How monetary excesses and shortages will be shared. Frequently matches possession.

Navigation — Techniques for going with significant business choices. May require consistent or larger part accomplice endorsement.

Accomplice Jobs and Obligations — Portrays the particular practical commitments and obligations of each accomplice.

Capital Commitments — Sum and type of resources put away by accomplices like money, property, hardware, and IP.

Withdrawal/Buyout Terms — Interaction in the event that an accomplice leaves, including value buyouts.

Clear organization arrangements forestall disarray not too far off as organizations develop and advance.

Investor Arrangements
Investor arrangements oversee relations between holders of organization stock. Comparative areas might include:

Proprietorship — Classes of offers held by every investor, number of offers, rates.

Share Move Limitations — Cutoff points on offering/moving offers to outcasts to keep up with control.

Profit Arrangements — Recipes for disseminating organization benefits as investor profits.

Casting a ballot Game plans — Techniques for investor gatherings and appointment of the Top managerial staff.

Defensive Arrangements — Minority investor securities against changes by the larger part.

Purchase Sell Arrangements — Interaction for share reclamations in the event that an investor leaves or passes away.

For partnerships, recording share assignment, freedoms, and administration forthright dodges issues later.

Working Arrangements

LLC working arrangements spread out guidelines and include:

Proprietorship Design — Rates possessed by every part. Can empower adaptable offer assignments.

Jobs and Obligations — Portrays part and director obligations if chief made due.

Capital Commitments — Characterizes part interests into the LLC at development.

Benefit/Deficit Conveyance — How net benefits or misfortunes will be designated to individuals.

Part Changes — Cycle for adding or eliminating individuals.

Direction — The board construction and casting a ballot systems.

Buyout Terms — How withdrawing individuals can reclaim their proprietorship interest.

This adaptability settles on working arrangements valuable for beginning phase adventures.

Venture Arrangements

Each subsidizing round requires a speculation arrangement overseeing:

Venture Sums — How much capital financial backers will give and achievements.

Protections Gave — Number and sort of possession shares given to financial backers.

Financial backer Freedoms — Casting a ballot, first refusal on future rounds, data access, and so on.

Limitations — Cutoff points on share moves and added new financial backers.

Reclamation Privileges — Terms for the startup repurchasing shares from financial backers.

Pay-to-Play Arrangements — Necessity that current financial backers take part in later adjusts.

Leave Privileges — Financial backer's possibilities for getting a profit from venture like selling shares.

All around organized speculation arrangements carry lucidity to startup gathering pledges.

Convertible Note Arrangements
Convertible note bargains are middle startup financing choices with:

Advance Sum — The chief sum gave to the startup through the note.

Financing cost + Development Date — Premium rate and date the advance proselytes to value or is reimbursed.

Change Markdown — Level of rebate on transformation share cost to boost change.

Valuation Cap — Most extreme valuation where note changes over. Financial backer assurance on the off chance that valuation is high.

Qualified Supporting — Next value round that triggers compulsory advance transformation while meeting set size.

Change of Control Proviso — Converts credit to shares assuming startup is procured before transformation.

Appropriately organized convertible notes permit new businesses to defer valuation discussions until future subsidizing adjusts.

Advance Arrangements
Taking out business advances requires formal credit arrangements specifying:

Credit Sum and Reason — Aggregate sum and endorsed business utilizes.

Financing cost and Charges — Rates can be fixed or variable. This might incorporate start charges.

Reimbursement Timetable — Month to month or other installment recurrence and terms. Elegance periods.

Guarantee — Asset(s) got as insurance the bank can seize on the off chance that credit terms are penetrated.

Credit Pledges — Lawfully restricting vows to meet monetary targets and give monetary data.

Speed increase Condition — Permits the moneylender to request full quick credit reimbursement for pledge breaks.

Individual Assurance — Expects business visionaries to ensure the business' exhibition actually.

Advance agreements warrant fastidious assessment to guarantee reasonableness and forestall individual risk.

Protected innovation Arrangements

IP contracts guarantee possession privileges to elusive resources like:

Brand name Authorizing — Gives restricted freedoms to utilize brand names/marking for stock, and so on.

Patent Authorizing — This permits one more party to use licensed developments and innovation.

Copyright Authorizing — Awards restricted privileges to replicate, disseminate, and show protected works.

Innovation Move — Moves proprietorship and commercialization freedoms for creations, programming, and so on.

Classification (NDA) — Requires outsiders to stay quiet.

IP Task — Moves IP possession privileges from individual makers to the business.

Sovereignty Arrangements — Gives progressing eminence installments to IP privileges holders from produced income.

Safeguard inventive resources and IP through ironclad arrangements.

Key Agreement Discussion Tips for Business people
While assessing contracts, remember these tips to reinforce your situation:

Set aside some margin for An expected level of effort — Read cautiously and research new terms prior to marking anything.

Recruit Legitimate Guidance — Have a legal advisor experienced with new companies survey significant arrangements whenever the situation allows.

Explain Questionable Language — Banner obscure provisions and push for explicit, quantifiable terms.

Frame Significant Dealbreakers — Know essential arrangements you won't think twice about.

Demand Bidirectional Changes — Don't promptly acknowledge uneven proposition. Arrange terms commonly useful to all gatherings.

Revise Unimportant Standard Provisos —
Modify templated agreements to accommodate
what is going on.

Add Leave Methodologies — Remember
reasonable end arrangements for long haul
contracts.

Completely understanding agreements
empowers more grounded talks. Try not to rush
the lawful subtleties!

CHAPTER 7:

Individuals Power: Building and Driving Winning Groups

As a pioneer, I have discovered that building a triumphant group isn't just about tracking down the perfect individuals with the right abilities. It's tied in with making a culture where each individual can flourish and add to the group's prosperity. What's more, one of the best ways of accomplishing this is by focusing on qualities over shortcomings.

The way to building a triumphant group is to make a gathering of people who can cooperate towards a shared objective. This requires something beyond selecting individuals with the right abilities and experience. It implies making a culture where everybody feels esteemed and has the chance to contribute their extraordinary assets.

Strengthening

A vital element of winning groups is strengthening. I frequently depict initiative as a coin with different sides. One side is strengthening. As a pioneer, you really want to enable your group by articulating the "why" of the mission and allowing the group to drive the "how." Strengthening is tied in with designating position to the group and moving so they can assume liability, simply decide, and begin carrying out moves toward accomplish the essential targets.

Engaging the group drives deftness and speed in direction, the two of which are basic to the progress of the mission. At Amazon, groups are enabled to accomplish the essential targets by being permitted to investigate various ways to "yes." [1] Colleagues are engaged to investigate thoughts inside the group, with different groups, and even look for numerous heroes across the association who will vouch for their thought.

The opposite side of a similar coin is responsibility.

Responsibility

Responsibility implies every individual from the group and the group all in all is liable for following through on their assignments and together accomplishing the group objectives and vital goals. Research shows that groups work best when the colleagues are responsible to one another. In the US Armed force, responsibility is primary: troopers are responsible to their sergeant and to one another. [2] They are supposed to take responsibility for assignments and put their heart, brain, and soul into them with the goal that they can finish the mission. To work with responsibility, you want to guarantee that the colleagues play a part and errand lucidity and every one of the assets and devices they should take care of their business.

Variety

The third key element of winning groups is variety across all components, including variety of thought, encounters, rank, orientation, race, age, and foundation, among others. As a pioneer, you should cultivate a culture of variety, value, consideration, and having a place in your group. The examination is perfectly clear that the more different the group, the more creative it is and the more equipped for driving outcomes. [3] When individuals who think distinctively and have integral abilities, viewpoints, and encounters meet up, they are more fit for tackling issues quicker and better.

Mental Security

Groups that appreciate mental security can flourish and convey staggering new bits of knowledge. As Harvard Teacher Amy Edmondson has expressed in her original exploration, groups that vibe mentally protected, by which they bring their credible self and convey uninhibitedly, perform better. [4] Imperative components of mental security are trust and straightforwardness. As a pioneer, you have an obligation to show others how its done by stretching out your trust to the group and imparting straightforwardly. Trust is the paste that associates convictions, thoughts, words, and activities that are put in the possession of someone else unafraid of being double-crossed. Straightforwardness is open, opportune, and straightforward correspondence among the colleagues.

Correspondence

Correspondence is basic and essential in winning groups. Powerful correspondence can assist with diminishing task project requirements running wild and stand by times, de-raise high-stress, high-risk conditions, and further develop colleague confidence and commitment. As a pioneer, you want to impart early and frequently with your colleagues. You should be clear, fresh, and reliable with both your composed and verbal correspondence. This will assist with setting a model for other colleagues to imitate and follow.

A key to effective correspondence is undivided attention, by which you center around the speaker, you don't intrude on them, and you draw in them by posing unconditional inquiries. In correspondence, it is fundamental to likewise focus on nonverbal prompts and what is left implied by groups.

Research shows that when colleagues feel associated with one another, they perform better. As a pioneer, you can begin by rehearsing sympathy and getting to know your colleagues, as a matter of fact. You can likewise work with such associations by setting out open doors for colleagues to investigate and distinguish things they share practically speaking during virtual or in-person group meetups. You can likewise assist with joining individuals connect through group tasks and tutor pairings.

Persistent Learning
The last key component in winning groups is the feeling of development of the singular colleagues and the group overall through

ceaseless learning. Groups that learn together stay together, and pioneers that don't persistently learn can't lead. As a pioneer, you initially need to set a model by embracing long lasting learning. You can then work with persistent advancing by building a culture of learning in your group and offering learning valuable open doors and encounters to each colleague, contingent upon their necessities and inclinations, and to the group all in all.

One of the best group building exercises that I have been utilizing is our group learning meetings, where the group catches on together quickly. I for the most part welcome an outer speaker to represent 30 minutes on a basic point and permit the excess 30 minutes for questions and replies. This is a powerful way for the group to advance together and from one another. You can likewise offer input to your colleagues, figure out their goals, and assist them with diagramming a way of learning and development.

Building winning groups expects that you encourage and develop 7 attributes of winning groups: strengthening, responsibility, variety, close to home security, correspondence, association, and consistent learning. Building groups that convey results is a workmanship and science. As a pioneer, you can begin with these basic components to fabricate the underpinnings of your triumphant group.

The Customary Methodology - Zeroing in on Shortcomings

Generally, while building a group, the emphasis has been on recognizing shortcomings and tending to them. This approach expects that the most effective way to further develop execution is by fixing what's going on. Nonetheless, this approach has a few limits.

To start with, it tends to be demotivating for colleagues to zero in on their shortcomings continually. Second, it very well may be tedious and costly to address every one of the shortcomings in a group. Third, it doesn't consider the extraordinary qualities that every individual brings to the group.

The Elective Methodology - Expanding on Qualities

A superior way to deal with building a triumphant group is to zero in on qualities. This implies distinguishing and utilizing each colleague's novel assets to make a culture of greatness. Rather than attempting to fix shortcomings, this approach looks to expand on what's as of now working.

Understanding the Significance of Qualities Based Authority

Qualities based initiative is an administration style that spotlights on boosting the qualities of each colleague. This approach perceives that every individual has special gifts and capacities that can add to the group's prosperity. By zeroing in on qualities, pioneers can make a culture of energy and commitment.

Recognizing and Utilizing Individual Qualities

The most important phase in building a group in view of qualities is to distinguish each colleague's assets. This should be possible through appraisals, meetings, and perception. Whenever qualities are recognized, they can be utilized to make a group that is more noteworthy than the amount of its parts.

The Advantages of Focusing on Qualities over Shortcomings

Focusing on qualities over shortcomings has a few advantages. To begin with, it makes a culture of inspiration and commitment. At the point when colleagues are urged to utilize their assets, they feel more roused and participated in their work. Second, it can prompt more elevated levels of execution. At the point when people are doing what they specialize in, they are bound to deliver great work. Third, it can further develop group elements. At the point when colleagues are urged to appreciate and esteem each other's assets, it can prompt better correspondence and cooperation.

Developing a Positive Work Culture

In the present exceptionally cutthroat business scene, cultivating a positive work culture is fundamental to the progress of any association. Organizations that perceive the significance of representative joy and put resources into developing a solid workplace can receive the rewards of expanded efficiency, further developed worker maintenance, and improved generally speaking execution. In this, I will dig into the significant connection between representative joy and efficiency, investigate the mental and physiological variables that support this association, and give noteworthy experiences to assist you with making a flourishing work culture that benefits both your workers and your association.

Grasping the Association Between Representative Joy and Efficiency

Worker Commitment

Cheerful representatives are bound to be taken part in their work, adding to a more powerful and imaginative workplace. Connected with representatives are more dedicated to their work liabilities and invest heavily in their work. This elevated feeling of pride and responsibility converts into expanded efficiency.

Decreased Pressure and Burnout

A positive work culture that focuses on representative prosperity assists with decreasing pressure and burnout. At the point when representatives feel esteemed, upheld, and associated with their association, they are better prepared to oversee business related stressors. Diminished feelings of anxiety lead to improved mental and actual wellbeing, which thusly, advances expanded efficiency.

Further developed Coordinated effort and Cooperation

Representative bliss frequently prompts a more cooperative and steady workplace. Cheerful representatives are bound to be cooperative individuals, cooperating to accomplish shared objectives. A strong group encourages open correspondence, prompting inventive arrangements and expanded efficiency.

Improved Mental Working

Bliss has been displayed to emphatically affect mental working, which incorporates memory, consideration, and critical thinking skills. At the point when workers are cheerful, they are more engaged, alert, and equipped for producing intelligent fixes. This improved mental presentation eventually prompts higher efficiency.

Expanded Representative Maintenance

A positive work culture that cultivates representative joy adds to higher worker standards for dependability. At the point when representatives feel satisfied and fulfilled in their jobs, they are less inclined to look for potential open doors somewhere else. Holding gifted representatives brings about diminished turnover costs and a more experienced, useful labor force.

Methodologies to Develop a Positive Work Culture

Encourage Open Correspondence

Empower open correspondence by making channels for representatives to share their considerations, thoughts, and concerns. Giving open doors to representatives to voice their viewpoints and feel appreciated adds to a more comprehensive workplace and fortifies the feeling of having a place.

Perceive and Reward Worker Accomplishments

Routinely recognizing and compensating representative achievements, both of all shapes and sizes, can lift everyone's spirits and inspiration. A straightforward thank you, a note of appreciation, or a little badge of acknowledgment can go quite far in causing workers to feel esteemed and appreciated.

Advance Balance between fun and serious activities

Urge representatives to keep a sound balance between fun and serious activities by offering adaptable work game plans and supporting individual and family responsibilities. This adds to worker satisfaction as well as lessens burnout and truancy.

Put resources into Worker Improvement

Giving open doors to individual and expert development exhibits your obligation to your representatives' prosperity. Putting resources into preparing and improvement projects can assist workers with feeling more certain and skillful in their jobs, prompting expanded work fulfillment and efficiency.

Make a Culture of Trust and Regard

Encouraging a climate of trust and regard is pivotal for a positive work culture. Support straightforwardness, genuineness, and responsibility among colleagues and pioneers, and treat every representative with respect and decency.

Support Actual Wellbeing and Health

Advancing a solid way of life can fundamentally add to worker joy and efficiency. Execute wellbeing drives, like nearby wellness offices, quality dinner choices, and wellbeing challenges, to urge representatives to focus on their actual wellbeing.

Support Psychological wellness and Profound Prosperity

Emotional well-being assumes a huge part in by and large worker bliss and efficiency. Offer assets and backing for psychological wellness, for example, Representative Help Projects (EAPs), stress the board studios, and care preparing, to assist workers with keeping up with profound prosperity.

Urge Distributed Acknowledgment

Making a culture where representatives perceive and value their companions' endeavors and achievements can additionally upgrade working environment joy. Carry out a companion acknowledgment program to cultivate a feeling of brotherhood and establish a climate where workers support and praise each other's victories.

Measure Representative Bliss and Address Concerns

Routinely evaluate worker satisfaction through reviews, input meetings, and one-on-one gatherings. Utilize this data to distinguish regions for development and carry out designated methodologies to address worker concerns and improve fulfillment.

Turn into a Guaranteed Corporate Wellbeing Subject matter expert

Now that you comprehend the significance of developing a positive work culture and its immediate connection to representative joy and efficiency, now is the ideal time to make a move. By turning into an Ensured Corporate Health Trained professional, you will acquire the information and devices important to carry out compelling wellbeing programs in your association.

Making a positive work culture that encourages representative joy is fundamental for the drawn out progress of any association. By executing the procedures framed in this article, you can develop a strong and comprehensive climate where representatives flourish, bringing about expanded efficiency, further developed worker maintenance, and upgraded in general execution. By putting resources into the prosperity of your labor force, you are eventually putting resources into the future outcome of your association.

Initiative Systems for Progress

As a pioneer, having center abilities that will assist you with succeeding is urgent. Pioneers ' seven fundamental abilities are capital designation, methodology, ceaseless improvement, enrolling, independent direction, basically assessing execution, and extremist association. These abilities are principal for any pioneer to accomplish their objectives and lead their group to progress.

Capital distribution is one of the fundamental abilities that a pioneer ought to have. It includes settling on informed conclusions about where to contribute assets to accomplish the most ideal result. A pioneer's capacity to designate assets really can essentially influence the association's prosperity. Essentially, system is another basic expertise that a pioneer should have. It includes putting forth objectives, creating plans, and settling on choices to accomplish those objectives. A pioneer's capacity to construct and execute an obvious procedure is urgent to their prosperity.

Nonstop improvement is another imperative expertise that a pioneer should have. It includes a promise to progressing learning and improvement for them as well as their group. Enlisting is likewise a pivotal expertise for a pioneer. It comprises in distinguishing and drawing in the right ability to the association. A pioneer's capacity to select really can assist with building a strong and fruitful group. Navigation, basically assessing execution, and revolutionary association are fundamental abilities each pioneer ought to have. These abilities permit pioneers to pursue informed choices, assess their group's presentation, and assemble solid organizations to accomplish their objectives.

Figuring out Initiative
The Significance of Administration

Initiative is significant to any association, whether a private venture or a huge company. As a pioneer, you guide your group towards accomplishing the association's objectives. You should have a few center abilities to be a viable pioneer, including capital designation, procedure, consistent improvement, selecting, navigation, basically assessing execution, and revolutionary organization.

Capital distribution is choosing where to contribute the association's assets. As a pioneer, you should obviously figure out the association's monetary objectives and designate assets likewise. This expertise is fundamental for guaranteeing the drawn out progress of the association.

System is one more basic expertise for any pioneer. You'll have to foster a reasonable vision for the association and make an arrangement to accomplish that vision. This includes examining the association's assets and shortcomings and distinguishing valuable open doors and dangers on the lookout.

Persistent improvement is continually assessing and working on the association's cycles and systems. As a pioneer, you should distinguish regions for development and carry out changes to upgrade the association's presentation.

Enlisting is one more fundamental expertise for any pioneer. You should have the option to recognize and draw in top ability to the association. This includes making serious areas of strength for a brand and creating viable enlistment methodologies.

Direction is a basic expertise for any pioneer. You should have the option to settle on informed choices rapidly and successfully. This includes examining information, taking into account every single imaginable choice, and gauging the advantages and disadvantages of every choice.

Basically assessing execution is the method involved with evaluating the association's exhibition and recognizing regions for development. As a pioneer, you should have the option to impartially assess execution and carry out changes to improve the association's viability.

We are framing key associations with different associations to accomplish shared objectives. As a pioneer, you should have the option to distinguish likely accomplices and foster viable organization systems.

Moreover, initiative is a basic part of any association, and having the center abilities of capital designation, procedure, ceaseless improvement, enlisting, direction, fundamentally assessing execution, and revolutionary organization is fundamental for progress. As a pioneer, you should be focused on creating and utilizing these abilities to direct your group towards accomplishing the association's objectives.

7 Significant Initiative Abilities

Center Ability 1: Technique

To be a viable pioneer, you should have the center ability of methodology. This includes creating convincing systems to accomplish long haul objectives. To do this, you should initially characterize your fantasy result. What do you need to achieve over the long haul? Whenever you have characterized your fantasy result, you should separate it into explicit objectives. This will assist you with making a guide to direct your excursion.

I believe it's crucial for survey and change your system depending on the situation consistently. This will guarantee that you remain focused and progress towards your objectives. As a pioneer, you should have the option to think basically and pursue difficult choices in regards to procedure.

To foster your abilities around here, think about concentrating on fruitful pioneers and their techniques. If it's not too much trouble, search for examples and best practices to integrate into your methodology.

Just to remind you, technique is certainly not a one-time occasion. A continuous cycle requires steady consideration and refinement.

Center Ability 2: Enrolling

Enrolling is a basic center expertise for any pioneer. To fabricate a fruitful group, you should fixate on tracking down ability. Develop positive, spurred, and motivating individuals who can give direction, responsibility, and new open doors. Here are a few fundamental tips to assist you with succeeding at selecting:

- Obviously characterize the abilities and characteristics you are searching for in a competitor. Make an expected set of responsibilities that frames the fundamental obligations and capabilities expected for the job.

- Utilize an assortment of obtaining techniques to track down expected competitors. Influence your own and proficient organizations, post work postings on pertinent work sheets, and utilize web-based entertainment to advance the position.

- Screen up-and-comers cautiously to guarantee they meet the capabilities for the job. Direct telephone and in-person meetings to evaluate their abilities, experience, and social fit.

- Ensure you are offering the chance to competitors. Feature the advantages of working for your association and why the job accommodates their vocation objectives.

- Give a positive competitor experience. Be responsive, straightforward, and proficient all through the enlistment interaction.

These tips can construct a gifted and spurred group to drive your association's prosperity.

Center Ability 3: Capital Portion

To be an effective pioneer, you should have center capital portion abilities. This expertise includes designating assets to amplify returns for your association. To do this successfully, you should initially recognize the main thing to you and your association. Whenever you have set your needs, you can mercilessly zero in on them.

One method for doing this is by making a table that frames your needs and the assets expected to accomplish them. This will assist you with arriving at informed conclusions about apportioning your assets. Furthermore, you ought to ceaselessly assess your decisions to guarantee that you are expanding returns.

It's critical to take note of that capital allotment isn't just about monetary assets. It additionally includes assigning your time, energy, and ability. As a pioneer, you should have the option to recognize the assets that are generally important to your association and give them as needs be.

In outline, capital distribution is a basic center expertise for any pioneer. By distinguishing the main thing to you, laying out boundaries, and savagely zeroing in on them, you can allot your assets to augment returns and drive accomplishment for your association.

Center Ability 4: Constant Improvement

Ceaseless improvement is an essential expertise for any pioneer. As a pioneer, you ought to constantly look for new information, secure new abilities, and curate new encounters to work on yourself and your group. This expertise includes an eagerness to master and adjust to new circumstances and a pledge to personal growth.

To constantly improve, you ought to zero in on recognizing regions where you can improve and putting forth objectives to accomplish those enhancements. This might include looking for criticism from others, dissecting your exhibition, or exploring to distinguish best practices.

One successful device for persistent improvement is the Effect Exertion Framework, which assesses the significance of any undertaking by effect and exertion. This dynamic apparatus can assist you with focusing on your endeavors and spotlight on the region with the main effect.

By persistently working on yourself and your group, you can remain in front of the opposition and make colossal hierarchical progress.

Center Ability 5: Navigation

As a pioneer, one of your center abilities is direction. You should pursued difficult choices to drive progress. To develop solid logical abilities, record basic decisions, think about expected dangers and prizes, and afterward fearlessly execute.

Viable direction requires a smart and methodical methodology. One method for moving toward direction is to utilize a critical thinking process like the 7-step or 5W1H technique. These strategies assist you with recognizing the issue, accumulate important data, dissect the information, and create and execute an answer.

Another supportive device is the Challenge model, which represents Information, Options, Dangers, and Assessment. This model aides you accumulate and examine information, create choices, assess possible dangers, and choose in view of the most ideal that anyone could hope to find data.

Recall that independent direction is tied in with settling on the ideal decision and unhesitatingly executing that decision. This requires compelling correspondence and administration abilities to guarantee everybody is energetic about the choice and realizes their part in carrying out it.

Center Ability 6: Assessing Execution

Basically assessing execution is a center expertise of a pioneer. To do this really, you should set clear estimates that line up with your objectives and consistently keep tabs on your development. Quit misleading yourself and live by the numbers. This will permit you to settle on information driven choices and recognize regions for development.

One method for assessing execution is by directing ordinary execution audits with your colleagues. This permits you to give input on their exhibition and distinguish regions for improvement. It likewise permits your colleagues to give input on your administration style and recommend regions for development.

One more method for assessing execution is by setting up a framework for following key execution pointers (KPIs). This permits you to screen progress towards your objectives and recognize regions to change. It additionally assists you with recognizing patterns and examples in your information, which can illuminate your direction.

As well as following KPIs, gathering input from your clients, partners, and other key partners is fundamental. This can assist you with distinguishing regions where you want to work on your items or administrations and where you can work on your correspondence and coordinated effort.

You can turn into a more powerful pioneer and drive your group towards progress by dominating assessing execution.

Center Ability 7: Joining forces with Partners

Cooperating with partners is vital as a pioneer to assist you with accomplishing your association's objectives. By building strong associations with every single important partner, including representatives, clients, providers, and financial backers, you can acquire significant experiences, cultivate trust, and make a common vision for progress.

To actually collaborate with partners, you should assume liability and take responsibility for activities. I figure you should conveyed straightforwardly and straightforwardly, listened effectively to criticism, and were able to adjust your methodology in view of the necessities and assumptions for your partners.

One method for further developing your partner interchanges is utilizing the RPM Announcement System. This structure includes considering your advancement, introducing your discoveries, and planning your subsequent stages. Following this cycle can keep partners educated and drew in and fabricate more grounded connections.

As well as building associations with partners, working intimately with your directorate is fundamental. By teaming up with your board, you can guarantee that your association is lined up with its essential objectives and has the assets and backing you really want to succeed.

Collaborating with partners is a center expertise that can assist you with accomplishing your initiative objectives. Building strong connections, looking for liability, and conveying really can make a culture of trust, straightforwardness, and shared achievement.

The Effect of Powerful Authority

As a pioneer, having the 7 center abilities examined in this focuses can fundamentally affect your group and association. Viable capital distribution can expand benefits and development, while a very much created system can give guidance and concentration. Persistent improvement guarantees that your group generally endeavors to improve, and selecting the perfect individuals can make a strong and proficient group.

Great direction can save time and assets, while basically assessing execution can distinguish improvement regions. At long last, revolutionary organizations can prompt creative arrangements and new open doors.

You can turn into a more viable pioneer by dominating these abilities, moving your group to accomplish their best, and driving your association towards progress.

CHAPTER 8:

Adjusting to Change: Flourishing in Unique Business sectors

In the present quickly changing business sector scene, organizations face serious rivalry, making it significant to foster compelling techniques to remain ahead. To take down your opposition and flourish in this powerful climate, it is vital for embrace change, advance, and adjust. In this, I will investigate key techniques that can assist you with taking down your opposition in business while exploring the developing economic situations.

Understanding the Significance of Adjusting to Economic situations

1. The business scene is continually developing, with economic situations assuming an essential part in deciding the achievement or

disappointment of associations. adjusting to these economic situations isn't simply an extravagance yet a need for organizations hoping to flourish in a cutthroat climate. In this part, we will dive into the significance of understanding and actually answering economic situations, and how SEC Structure S-2 methodologies can assist organizations with remaining on the ball.

2. One of the key justifications for why adjusting to economic situations is fundamental is that it empowers organizations to remain applicable. Markets are dynamic, and shopper inclinations, industry patterns, and financial elements can change quickly. Neglecting to adjust to these progressions can bring about a deficiency of portion of the overall industry and at last, business disappointment. Take the case of Kodak, a once-industry goliath that neglected to adjust to the shift from film to computerized photography. Regardless of holding licenses for computerized camera innovation, Kodak's hesitance to embrace the changing economic situations prompted its destruction.

3. Adjusting to economic situations likewise permits organizations to exploit arising open doors. By intently checking market patterns and shopper requests, associations can recognize new areas of development and foster imaginative items or administrations to address those issues. Netflix, for example, perceived the rising notoriety of web based streaming and adjusted its plan of action from DVD rentals to a real time feature, making it a prevailing player in media outlets.

4. To really adjust to economic situations, organizations need to accumulate and dissect significant information. This can include directing statistical surveying, checking contenders, and remaining informed about industry patterns. By utilizing information driven bits of knowledge, associations can settle on informed choices and foster procedures that line up with market requests. For instance, Coca-Cola presented Coca-Cola Zero Sugar in

the wake of recognizing a developing purchaser inclination for better drink choices.

5. One more significant part of adjusting to economic situations is adaptability. Organizations that are unbending and impervious to change frequently battle to get by in powerful business sectors. Then again, organizations that embrace adaptability can rapidly change their techniques and activities to line up with advancing economic situations. An outstanding contextual investigation is Nokia, which at first overwhelmed the cell phone industry however neglected to adjust to the ascent of cell phones. Conversely, Apple perceived the changing economic situations and effectively sent off the iPhone, moving the organization higher than ever.

6. At long last, organizations can use SEC Structure S-2 methodologies to adjust to economic situations and gain an upper hand. This structure is utilized by organizations to enlist protections contributions with the U.S.

protections and Trade commission (SEC). By concentrating on the data revealed in SEC Structure S-2 filings of contenders and industry pioneers, organizations can acquire important experiences into their techniques, monetary execution, and market situating. This information can illuminate navigation and assist associations with adjusting their own methodologies as needs be.

7. All in all, adjusting to economic situations is imperative for organizations to stay pertinent, take advantage of chances, and support achievement. By understanding the significance of market transformation and utilizing procedures, for example, SEC structure S-2 investigation, associations can explore the consistently changing business scene with certainty and dexterity. Remain tuned for the following area, where we will investigate commonsense tips and best practices for actually adjusting to economic situations utilizing SEC Structure S-2 procedures.

Understanding the Significance of Adjusting to Market Elements

1. Understanding the Significance of Adjusting to Market Elements

In the present quickly changing business scene, it is pivotal for organizations to remain on the ball by adjusting to advertise elements. Market elements allude to the powers and factors that influence the organic market of labor and products, as well as the generally serious scene. These elements can be impacted by different variables, including monetary circumstances, mechanical headways, customer inclinations, and administrative changes, among others. Neglecting to perceive and answer these market elements can prompt botched open doors, diminished seriousness, and even business disappointment.

2. The effect of Market elements on Evaluating Techniques

One region where market elements have a critical effect is estimating systems. Conventional fixed valuing models may not be compelling in the present unique business sectors, as they don't consider adaptability in light of evolving conditions. basing point estimating, then again, offers a more versatile methodology. This valuing methodology sets a gauge cost for an item or administration, which can be changed in view of changes in economic situations, for example, transportation expenses, duties, or taxes.

3. The advantages of Basing Point evaluating Adaptability

Basing point estimating adaptability gives a few benefits to organizations. Right off the bat, it permits organizations to answer rapidly to changes in costs, guaranteeing that costs stay cutthroat. For instance, on the off chance that transportation costs increment because of rising fuel costs, an organization utilizing basing point valuing can change their costs likewise, keeping up with benefit while as yet offering cutthroat costs to clients.

4. Correlation: Basing Point Estimating versus Fixed Estimating

To all the more likely comprehend the advantages of basing point estimating adaptability, how about we contrast it with conventional fixed evaluating. Fixed estimating, as the name recommends, sets a static cost for an item or administration, paying little mind to changes in economic situations. While fixed evaluating might give solidness, it comes up short on versatility expected to answer market elements. Therefore, organizations utilizing fixed valuing might wind up in a difficult spot while confronting cost variances or changes in client interest.

5. True Models

To outline the adequacy of basing point valuing adaptability, how about we think about two speculative situations. In Situation A, an organization utilizing fixed estimating sets their item cost at $10 per unit. Notwithstanding, because of a surprising expansion in unrefined substance costs, their overall revenues therapist, and they can't change their costs to redress. Subsequently, they might confront monetary troubles or need to reduce expenses somewhere else.

Conversely, in Situation B, an organization utilizing basing point estimating sets their standard cost at $10 per unit however changes it in light of changes in market elements. At the point when unrefined substance costs increment, they can raise their costs in like manner to keep up with productivity. This adaptability permits them to explore market variances actually and guarantee their business stays maintainable.

Understanding and adjusting to advertise elements is critical for organizations to flourish in the present cutthroat scene. Basing point estimating adaptability offers a significant device for organizations to answer changes in costs and stay serious. By taking into account the advantages and downsides of various valuing methodologies, organizations can settle on informed choices and position themselves for progress in a powerful commercial center.

Understanding the Significance of Adjusting to Market Patterns

In the realm of business, each business person expects to find true success. Nonetheless, business achievement doesn't come simple, and business visionaries should have the option to adjust to advertise patterns to remain in front of the opposition. In the present business world, market patterns are continually advancing, and the people who can't or will not adjust to these progressions risk falling behind. Adjusting to showcase patterns is critical for organizations to stay significant and serious, and it can prompt better yields on speculation (return for money invested) capital.

To begin, we should investigate what market patterns are. Market patterns allude to the overall course where a market is moving, in view of shopper conduct, inclinations, ways of managing money, and different variables. These patterns can be impacted by various outside factors, like changes in innovation, governmental issues, or the economy. As an entrepreneur, it means quite a bit to watch out for these patterns, as they can influence your industry and your objective market.

Here are a few central issues to remember with regards to the significance of adjusting to showcase patterns:

1. Remaining Pertinent: In the present high speed business world, remaining significant is essential. By keeping awake to-date on market patterns, you can guarantee that your business is offering items or administrations that are popular. For instance, on the off chance that you're running an eatery, you might have to adjust your menu to incorporate more veggie lover or sans gluten choices, as these are as of now famous patterns in the food business.

2. Addressing Client Needs: By adjusting to showcase patterns, you can meet the changing necessities of your clients. For instance, assuming you're running an online business store, you might have to offer free transportation or impromptu conveyance to stay aware of the opposition. By addressing your clients' requirements, you can fabricate an unwavering client base and increment your return for money invested capital.

3. remaining In front of the opposition: Adjusting to showcase patterns can give you an upper hand. By being quick to present another item or administration, you can draw in additional clients and increment your piece of the pie. For instance, when Macintosh presented the iPod, they were quick to offer a versatile music player that could store great many melodies. This gave them a tremendous benefit over their rivals and assisted with laying out them as a market chief.

4. Expanding return on initial capital investment Capital: Adjusting to advertise patterns can prompt more significant yields on venture capital. By offering items or administrations that are popular, you can build your deals and benefits. For instance, on the off chance that you're running a skincare organization, you might have to present another line of items that are centered around hostile to maturing, as this is an emerging trend in the luxury industry. Thusly, you can build your return for money invested capital and develop your business.

Adjusting to showcase patterns is significant for organizations to stay serious and effective. By keeping awake to-date on market patterns, addressing client needs, remaining in front of the opposition, and expanding return on initial capital investment capital, organizations can situate themselves for long haul achievement.

Understanding the Significance of Adjusting to Market Patterns

To prevail in the venture world, it is significant to comprehend and successfully answer market patterns. Market patterns can fundamentally affect returns, as they drive interest, shape purchaser conduct, and impact market elements. Adjusting to these patterns permits financial backers to situate their portfolios decisively and make the most of arising open doors. Neglecting to adjust can bring about botched open doors, stale development, and, surprisingly, huge misfortunes.

Understanding the Significance of Adjusting to Economic situations

In the present quickly developing business scene, one of the key factors that can decide the achievement or disappointment of an organization is its capacity to adjust to economic situations. Economic situations allude to the different elements that impact the interest and supply of items or administrations in a specific market. These variables can remember changes for purchaser inclinations, monetary circumstances, innovative headways, and serious tensions, among others.

Adjusting to economic situations is pivotal in light of the fact that it permits organizations to remain applicable and serious in a steadily evolving climate. By getting it and answering business sector patterns, organizations can distinguish new open doors, moderate dangers, and streamline their profit from speculation (return for money invested). How about we investigate this further for certain models, tips, and contextual analyses.

Model: Consider an organization that produces cell phones. On the off chance that the market pattern shows a shift towards bigger screen measures, the organization should adjust its item contributions to satisfy this need. By presenting cell phones with bigger screens, the organization can draw in additional clients and increment its piece of the pie.

Tip: Routinely screen and examine market information to distinguish arising patterns and changes in customer conduct. This should be possible through statistical surveying, client studies, and online entertainment tuning in. By remaining informed, organizations can proactively adjust their methodologies to line up with economic situations.

Contextual investigation: Netflix is a great representation of an organization that effectively adjusted to changing economic situations. Initially a DVD rental help, Netflix perceived the developing interest for internet web based and moved its plan of action in like manner. By putting resources into content creation and circulation, the organization turned into a main player in the streaming business, outperforming conventional digital television suppliers.

All in all, adjusting to economic situations is fundamental for organizations to flourish in the present powerful commercial center. By understanding the significance of remaining coordinated and receptive to evolving patterns, organizations can situate themselves for long haul achievement. Whether it's through item development, key organizations, or functional changes, adjusting to economic situations is a critical part of boosting return on initial capital investment and keeping an upper hand.

Understanding the Significance of Adjusting to Economic situations

In the present always impacting business world, it is critical for organizations to adjust to economic situations to stay cutthroat and fruitful. adjusting to economic situations is the most common way of changing business procedures, items, and administrations in light of changes on the lookout. Inability to adjust could bring about diminished deals, loss of piece of the pie, and at last, business disappointment. Understanding the significance of adjusting to economic situations is the most vital phase in fostering an effective business procedure.

1. The Significance of Adjusting to Economic situations

Adjusting to economic situations is significant because of multiple factors. It, first and foremost, permits organizations to stay significant and serious on the lookout. As economic situations change, buyer inclinations and necessities change too. By adjusting to these changes, organizations can guarantee that they are addressing the necessities of their clients and giving items and administrations that are sought after. This can prompt expanded deals and portion of the overall industry.

2. Adjusting to Economic situations through Move forward Leases

One way that organizations can adjust to economic situations is through move forward leases. A move forward rent is a rent understanding in which the lease increments after some time. This sort of rent can be valuable for organizations that are simply beginning or are uncertain of their drawn out needs. By beginning with a lower lease and continuously expanding it over the long haul, organizations can change their costs as their income develops.

3. Examination of Move forward Leases to Other Rent Choices

While move forward leases can be a decent choice for certain organizations, it means quite a bit to contrast them with other rent choices to figure out which is ideal. For instance, a conventional rent with a decent lease might be a superior choice for organizations that have a steady income stream. Then again, a month-to-month rent might be a superior choice for organizations that are uncertain of their drawn out needs.

4. Instances of Fruitful Variation to Economic situations

There are numerous instances of organizations that have effectively adjusted to economic situations. One model is Netflix, what began as a DVD rental help yet moved its concentration to spilling as buyer inclinations changed. One more model is Amazon, what began as a web-based book shop yet extended to offer many items and administrations in light of changing economic situations.

5. End

Adjusting to economic situations is critical for organizations that need to stay cutthroat and effective. Move forward leases can be a decent choice for organizations that are simply beginning or are uncertain of their drawn out needs, yet it means quite a bit to contrast them with other rent choices to figure out which is ideal. By understanding the significance of adjusting to economic situations and doing whatever it takes to do as such, organizations can guarantee their drawn out progress.

Understanding the Significance of Adjusting to Economic situations

In the present speedy business climate, it is pivotal for organizations to have the option to adjust and answer economic situations really. Economic situations are continually changing, and organizations should remain on the ball to stay serious and flourish. Adjusting to economic situations includes grasping the present status of the market, distinguishing patterns and moves, and changing techniques and strategies appropriately. This part plans to reveal insight into the meaning of adjusting to economic situations and give bits of knowledge on how organizations can successfully explore through the always changing business scene.

1. Staying aware of customer requests: One of the essential explanations behind adjusting to economic situations is to satisfy the consistently developing needs of buyers. Shopper inclinations and necessities are consistently changing, affected by elements like innovation progressions, financial movements, and cultural patterns. By remaining on top of these changes, organizations can tailor their items, administrations, and advertising endeavors to line up with what clients need. For instance, consider a dress retailer that sees a developing pattern towards feasible and eco-accommodating style. By adjusting their item contributions to incorporate more manageable choices, they can draw in and hold clients who focus on moral utilization.

2. Jumping all over chances and limiting dangers: Adjusting to economic situations permits organizations to profit by arising amazing open doors while limiting expected chances. By intently observing business sector patterns and moves, organizations can recognize new specialties, undiscovered business sectors, or arising advances that can prompt development and extension. Then again, neglecting to adjust can leave organizations powerless against market interruptions and monetary slumps. For example, during the Coronavirus pandemic, numerous eateries immediately adjusted by offering takeout and conveyance choices to endure the limitations on eat in administrations. The individuals who neglected to adjust experienced huge misfortunes or even needed to close their entryways for all time.

3. remaining in front of the opposition: In a serious market, organizations should continually endeavor to separate themselves from their rivals. Adjusting to economic situations empowers organizations to remain in front of the opposition by being proactive and receptive to changing client needs. By offering imaginative items, prevalent client care, or one of a kind offers, organizations can draw in and hold clients, even in soaked markets. For instance, consider the cell phone industry, where organizations like Apple and Samsung constantly adjust their items to fulfill customer needs for quicker processors, better cameras, and further developed battery duration.

4. improving long haul maintainability: Adjusting to economic situations isn't just about transient endurance yet additionally about long haul manageability. Organizations that neglect to adjust risk becoming outdated and losing their significance on the lookout. By embracing change and constantly developing, organizations can situate themselves for long haul achievement. This might include putting resources into innovative work, cultivating a culture of development, or investigating new plans of action. For example, Blockbuster, when a predominant player in the video rental industry, neglected to adjust to the ascent of web based web-based features like Netflix. Therefore, they lost their upper hand and eventually failed.

Understanding the significance of adjusting to economic situations is pivotal for the achievement and endurance of organizations. By staying aware of purchaser requests, taking advantage of chances, remaining in front of the opposition, and improving long haul maintainability, organizations can explore through the powerful business scene actually. Adjusting to economic situations is definitely not a one-time task however a continuous interaction that requires constant observing, investigation, and vital independent direction. Simply by embracing change and being adaptable could organizations at any point flourish in a consistently evolving market.

Understanding the Significance of Adjusting to Market Patterns

Understanding the significance of adjusting to advertise patterns is vital for organizations to remain ahead in the present quickly changing business scene. Market patterns allude to the movements and changes in customer inclinations, industry elements, mechanical headways, and financial circumstances that influence the interest and supply of items or administrations. Adjusting to these patterns is fundamental for organizations to stay cutthroat, draw in clients, and drive development.

According to a client's point of view, adjusting to showcase patterns implies giving them items or administrations that line up with their developing necessities and inclinations. For instance, as manageability turns into an inexorably significant worry for shoppers, organizations need to adjust by offering eco-accommodating other options or integrating reasonable practices into their tasks. Thusly, they meet client assumptions as well as separate themselves from contenders.

From a business outlook, adjusting to showcase patterns permits organizations to profit by arising valuable open doors and relieve expected chances. By intently checking market patterns, organizations can recognize new specialties or undiscovered business sectors where they can grow their contributions. For example, the ascent of remote work during the Coronavirus pandemic spurred an interest for work space furniture and gear. Organizations fast to adjust exploited this pattern by presenting new product offerings or changing existing ones to take special care of the developing distant labor force.

To additionally comprehend the significance of adjusting to advertise patterns, think about the accompanying focuses:

1. Upper hand: Adjusting to showcase patterns empowers organizations to acquire an upper hand over their opponents. By remaining receptive to changing client inclinations and industry elements, organizations can foster inventive arrangements that satisfy developing needs before their rivals do.

2. Consumer loyalty: Adjusting to advertise patterns guarantees that organizations keep on gathering client assumptions and convey esteem. By understanding what clients need and need at some random time, organizations can tailor their contributions appropriately, prompting more elevated levels of consumer loyalty and faithfulness.

3. Business Development: Adjusting to advertise patterns opens up new roads for development and extension. By distinguishing arising patterns right off the bat, organizations can situate themselves as industry pioneers and catch a bigger piece of the pie. This can bring about expanded income, benefit, and long haul maintainability.

4. Risk Moderation: Adjusting to showcase patterns assists organizations with relieving potential dangers related with changes in customer conduct or financial circumstances. By broadening their item contributions or entering new business sectors in light of arising patterns, organizations can diminish their dependence on a solitary item or market, making them stronger to changes popular.

Understanding the significance of adjusting to showcase patterns is crucial for organizations expecting to remain ahead in the present serious business.

Embracing Development

Why Development is Critical for Business Development?

Development is the backbone of any business. It is the way to opening new open doors, working on existing items and administrations, and remaining in front of contenders. In the present quick moving, steadily changing business climate, development is as of now not an extravagance, however a need. Without it, organizations risk becoming insignificant, losing portion of the overall industry, and eventually, coming up short. In this segment, we will investigate why development is essential for business development, and how organizations might encourage a culture of development.

1. Advancement drives development

The fact that drives business development makes progression the motor. By persistently advancing, organizations can foster new items and administrations that meet the changing requirements and assumptions for their clients. This can prompt expanded deals, piece of the pie, and productivity. For instance, Apple's presentation of the iPhone upset the cell phone industry and moved the organization to become one of the most significant on the planet.

2. Advancement further develops proficiency

Development can likewise assist organizations with working on their effectiveness and diminish costs. By growing new cycles or advancements, organizations can smooth out their tasks and increment efficiency. For instance, Amazon's utilization of mechanical technology in its satisfaction habitats has permitted the organization to handle orders all the more rapidly and productively, diminishing the time and cost of conveyance.

3. Development upgrades client experience

Development can likewise upgrade the client experience by giving better than ever items and administrations. By expecting client needs and inclinations, organizations can make items and administrations that surpass assumptions and construct faithfulness. For instance, Netflix's presentation of its web-based feature changed the manner in which individuals consume diversion, giving a more helpful and customized insight for clients.

4. Development cultivates a culture of imagination

Development requires imagination and an eagerness to face challenges. By cultivating a culture of inventiveness, organizations can urge workers to produce groundbreaking thoughts and arrangements. This can prompt a more connected with and inspired labor force, as well as a pipeline of new items and administrations. For instance, Google's popular "20% time" strategy permits representatives to go through one day seven days chipping away at their own ventures, prompting advancements, for example, Google Guides and Gmail.

5. Advancement is fundamental for endurance

In the present quickly changing business climate, development is fundamental for endurance. Organizations that neglect to develop risk becoming out of date, as contenders present new items and administrations that meet changing client needs and inclinations. For instance, Kodak's inability to adjust to the computerized photography transformation prompted its liquidation in 2012.

Advancement is vital for business development and endurance. By driving development, further developing proficiency, improving client experience, cultivating a culture of imagination, and remaining in front of contenders, organizations can flourish in the present powerful business climate. To cultivate a culture of development, organizations ought to energize imagination, embrace risk-taking, and put resources into innovative work. Thusly, they can guarantee that they stay significant and serious in the years to come.

The Advantages of Embracing Development in Your Business

Development is crucial for the development and progress of any business. Embracing groundbreaking thoughts, innovations, and approaches can assist associations with remaining in front of the opposition, further develop effectiveness and efficiency, and increment productivity. In this part, we will investigate a portion of the advantages of embracing development in your business.

1. Expanded Proficiency and Efficiency

Development can assist your business with smoothing out activities, computerize processes, and lessen squander. By embracing new advances and approaches, you can take out tedious manual assignments and speed up. For instance, utilizing cloud-based programming can assist you with mechanizing your bookkeeping processes, while putting resources into new apparatus can assist you with accelerating creation.

2. Further developed Client Experience

Advancement can likewise assist you with improving the client experience. By embracing new advancements and approaches, you can offer your clients more customized and custom-made encounters. For instance, utilizing information investigation can assist you with bettering grasp your clients' requirements and inclinations, permitting you to offer them more designated items and administrations.

3. Expanded Adaptability

Advancement can likewise assist your business with turning out to be more adaptable and versatile. By embracing novel thoughts and approaches, you can answer all the more rapidly to changing economic situations and client needs. For instance, on the off chance that you are a retailer, you can utilize information investigation to rapidly distinguish drifts and change your item contributions in like manner.

4. Upper hand

Development can give your business an upper hand. By embracing groundbreaking thoughts and advances, you can separate yourself from your rivals and deal your clients one of a kind items and administrations. For instance, on the off chance that you are an eatery, you can utilize computer generated reality to offer your clients a special feasting experience.

5. Expanded Productivity

At long last, development can assist your business with expanding productivity. By embracing new advancements and approaches, you can diminish costs, increment effectiveness, and create new income streams. For instance, in the event that you are a producer, you can utilize 3D printing to diminish creation expenses and proposition custom items to your clients.

Embracing advancement is crucial for the development and outcome of any business. By embracing novel thoughts, innovations, and approaches, you can expand effectiveness and efficiency, further develop the client experience, become more adaptable and versatile, gain an upper hand, and increment productivity. In this way, feel free to attempt new things and embrace advancement in your business.

How to Cultivate a Culture of Development in Your Association?

Perhaps of the main test associations face is encouraging a culture of development. It's sufficiently not to have a couple of creative workers; development should be a piece of the association's DNA. It requires a change in outlook and a readiness to face challenges. In this segment, we'll investigate various ways of building a culture of development in your association.

1. energize Hazard taking

Development is tied in with facing challenges, and a culture that empowers risk-taking is fundamental. Workers need to have a solid sense of reassurance to face challenges unafraid of disappointment or retaliation. Urge representatives to examination and attempt new things. Celebrate disappointments as well as triumphs, and gain from them. Make a culture where disappointment is viewed as a venturing stone to progress.

2. Encourage Cooperation

Development is certainly not a performance try. It requires cooperation and collaboration. Urge cross-utilitarian groups to cooperate on projects. Give open doors to workers to share thoughts and conceptualize. Make a culture where everybody's thoughts are esteemed, no matter what their situation in the association.

3. Enable Representatives

Advancement can't be constrained; it necessities to come from the inside. Engage workers to drive advancement by giving them the assets they need. Give them the opportunity to investigate groundbreaking thoughts and take responsibility for projects. Urge them to take on new difficulties and stretch their capacities.

4. Give Preparing and Advancement

Development requires abilities and information. Give preparing and improvement amazing open doors to representatives to assist them with building their development abilities. Urge them to go to gatherings and studios, and give them admittance to web based learning assets. Put resources into their turn of events, and they will put resources into the association's prosperity.

5. Reward Development

Development ought to be perceived and compensated. Make a culture where workers are perceived for their inventive thoughts and commitments. Give impetuses and rewards to fruitful tasks. Praise victories and offer them with the whole association.

6. Embrace Variety

Development flourishes in different conditions. Energize variety and inclusivity in the association. Make a culture where everybody's thoughts are esteemed, no matter what their experience or experience. Embrace alternate points of view and use them to drive advancement.

Encouraging a culture of development requires a change in outlook and an eagerness to face challenges. Energize risk-taking, encourage joint effort, engage workers, give preparing and improvement, reward advancement, and embrace variety. By following these means, you can fabricate a culture of development in your association and drive development and achievement.

The Job of Innovation in Driving Development

The job of Innovation in Driving advancement

Innovation has turned into a fundamental piece of our regular routines, upsetting the manner in which we live, work, and convey. With the headways in innovation, development has become more open and feasible. The job of innovation in driving advancement couldn't possibly be more significant, as it has opened up additional opportunities, made new business sectors, and empowered organizations to remain serious. In this segment, we will investigate the various ways innovation drives advancement and its effect on organizations and society.

1. Empowering Coordinated effort and Innovativeness

Joint effort and innovativeness are basic parts of advancement. Innovation has made it more straightforward for people and groups to team up, no matter what their area. With the assistance of virtual gathering apparatuses, online undertaking the board frameworks, and cloud-based stages, groups can cooperate consistently, share thoughts, and trade input. This has prompted the development of new inventive items and administrations that could never have been conceivable without the coordinated effort and imagination empowered by innovation.

2. Giving Admittance to Data and Information

Admittance to data and information is fundamental for development. Innovation has made it simpler to store, examine, and share information, furnishing organizations with significant experiences that can drive advancement. With the assistance of enormous information investigation instruments, organizations can recognize examples, patterns, and client conduct, prompting the formation of new items and administrations that take care of the requirements of buyers.

3. Computerizing Cycles and Assignments

Computerization is a strong driver of development. Innovation has empowered organizations to computerize routine undertakings, saving time and assets for additional imaginative and inventive pursuits. Computerization has additionally prompted the advancement of new items and administrations, for example, chatbots, menial helpers, and self-driving vehicles, which are meaningfully altering the manner in which we live and work.

4. Engaging Clients and Buyers

Innovation has engaged clients and purchasers, empowering them to get to data, look at items and administrations, and settle on informed choices. This has prompted the development of new plans of action, for example, the sharing economy, which depends on innovation to associate suppliers and purchasers. Innovation has likewise empowered organizations to customize their items and administrations, furnishing clients with a more customized insight.

The Significance of Coordinated effort and Variety in Development

Development is a vital component in driving development and progress in any industry. A fundamental apparatus permits organizations to remain serious, adjust to changing economic situations, and meet the developing necessities of their clients. In any case, development is definitely not a one-individual work. It requires cooperation and variety to make progress. In this part, we will investigate the significance of coordinated effort and variety in advancement.

Cooperation is the method involved with cooperating to accomplish a shared objective.

Coordinated effort in advancement includes uniting individuals with various abilities, encounters, and viewpoints to create novel thoughts and foster imaginative arrangements. Cooperation takes into account the pooling of assets and information, which can prompt forward leaps that probably won't have been imaginable in any case.

1. Coordinated effort cultivates innovativeness and development

Joint effort permits people to run thoughts by one another, prompting the making of additional inventive arrangements. The variety of viewpoints inside a cooperative group can assist with recognizing vulnerable sides and lead to a more thorough comprehension of the main concern. This, thus, can prompt more inventive and creative arrangements.

2. Cooperation lessens risk

Development is an unsafe business. Teaming up with others can diminish the gamble of disappointment by spreading the gamble across a gathering. Teaming up with others likewise considers the sharing of ability and assets, which can assist with alleviating gambles.

Variety is one more fundamental part of advancement. Variety alludes to the distinctions in race, orientation, age, nationality, culture, and training that exist inside a group. Variety brings a scope of viewpoints, encounters, and information to the table, which can prompt more inventive arrangements.

1. Variety advances development

Variety can prompt a more extensive scope of thoughts and viewpoints, which can prompt more inventive arrangements. People from various foundations and societies can offer exceptional perspectives and encounters that would be useful, which can prompt more exhaustive critical thinking.

2. Variety further develops navigation

Different groups can go with better choices since they have a more extensive scope of points of view and encounters to draw from. This can prompt better-informed choices that consider a scope of variables that could have been neglected by a less different group.

Cooperation and variety are fundamental parts of advancement. Uniting individuals with various abilities, encounters, and points of view can prompt more imaginative and inventive arrangements. Working together with others can decrease the gamble of disappointment and take into consideration the sharing of assets and ability. Variety can prompt a more extensive scope of thoughts and viewpoints, which can further develop navigation and advance development. By embracing cooperation and variety, organizations can make a culture of development that drives development and progress.

Normal Difficulties and Arrangements

Development is the soul of progress. It's the main thrust behind each business, association, and industry. Be that as it may, in spite of its significance, advancement can be hard to accomplish. There are various boundaries that can keep organizations from improving, going from absence of assets to an apprehension about disappointment. Defeating these hindrances is fundamental to remain in front of the opposition and flourish in the present high speed business world. In this segment, we'll investigate the absolute most normal difficulties to development and the arrangements that can assist organizations with defeating them.

1. Absence of Assets

One of the main boundaries to development is an absence of assets. Advancement calls for investment, cash, and skill, which can all be hard to come by for some organizations. At the point when assets are scant, it's not difficult to fall into the snare of zeroing in on momentary objectives as opposed to long haul development. Be that as it may, this approach can be heartbreaking over the long haul.

Arrangement: Focus on Development

To beat this hindrance, organizations should focus on development. This implies distributing assets explicitly for development and making it a piece of the organization's general system. It might likewise mean collaborating with different associations to share assets or putting resources into new advances that can smooth out activities and let loose assets for development.

2. Apprehension about Disappointment

Apprehension about disappointment is one more typical boundary to development. Numerous organizations are reluctant to face challenges or attempt new things since they're anxious about coming up short. This dread can prompt stagnation and an absence of progress.

Arrangement: Embrace Disappointment

To beat this hindrance, organizations should embrace disappointment. This implies making a culture that empowers trial and error and gaining from botches. It likewise implies furnishing representatives with the help and assets they need to face challenges and attempt new things.

3. Absence of Variety

An absence of variety can likewise be a boundary to development. At the point when everybody in a group thinks and acts the same way, it very well may be challenging to concoct groundbreaking thoughts and approaches.

Arrangement: Embrace Variety

To beat this hindrance, organizations should embrace variety. This implies recruiting individuals from various foundations and with alternate points of view. It likewise implies making a culture that qualities and supports variety of thought and thoughts.

4. Protection from Change

Protection from change is one more typical boundary to development. Many individuals are OK with business as usual and are reluctant to embrace groundbreaking thoughts and approaches.

Arrangement: Convey the Advantages

To conquer this boundary, organizations should impart the advantages of development. This implies making sense of how development can help the organization develop and flourish over the long haul. It likewise implies giving representatives the help they need to adjust to change and embrace groundbreaking thoughts.

5. Absence of Coordinated effort

At last, an absence of coordinated effort can be a boundary to development. At the point when various offices or groups inside an organization don't cooperate, it very well may be hard to share thoughts and concocted new methodologies.

Arrangement: Cultivate Cooperation

To conquer this hindrance, organizations should encourage coordinated effort. This implies separating storehouses and empowering cross-practical groups to cooperate. It likewise implies making a culture that qualities and prizes cooperation and collaboration.

Advancement is fundamental for organizations that need to remain in front of the opposition and flourish in the present quick moving business world. Nonetheless, there are various hindrances that can keep organizations from advancing. By focusing on development, embracing disappointment, embracing variety, imparting the advantages of advancement, and encouraging joint effort, organizations can beat these obstructions and accomplish the advancement they need to succeed.

Making a move to Embrace Development in Your Business

Advancement is basic to the outcome of any business, no matter what the business or size. Nonetheless, it isn't sufficient to recognize the significance of advancement just. To genuinely embrace development, organizations should make a move. This implies making a culture of development, putting resources into new innovations, and empowering imagination and trial and error.

1. Making a Culture of Development

Quite possibly of the main stage a business can take to embrace development is to make a culture that cultivates innovativeness and energizes trial and error. This implies enabling representatives to recommend groundbreaking thoughts, giving assets to advancement, and compensating risk-taking and trial and error.

For instance, Google is known for its imaginative culture. The organization has a strategy that permits representatives to spend up to 20% of their time dealing with projects that are not aspect of their responsibilities portrayal. This empowers imagination and trial and error, and has prompted the improvement of a portion of Google's best items, like Gmail and Google Guides.

2. Putting resources into New Advancements

One more significant stage in embracing advancement is to put resources into new advances. This could mean taking on new programming or equipment, or putting resources into innovative work.

For instance, numerous organizations are putting resources into man-made consciousness (simulated intelligence) and AI advancements.

These advances can assist organizations with robotizing undertakings, further develop client care, and gain experiences into client conduct. By putting resources into these advancements, organizations can remain on the ball and stay cutthroat in their industry.

3. Empowering Imagination and Trial and error

At long last, organizations should support inventiveness and trial and error to embrace development genuinely. This implies giving assets and backing to workers to attempt new things, and remunerating the people who face challenges and think of creative thoughts.

For instance, Amazon has a program called "Get it done" that urges representatives to attempt new things and investigation with novel thoughts. The organization likewise has a strategy that permits workers to try out novel plans to senior initiative, no matter what their situation inside the organization. This cultivates a culture of development and urges representatives to break new ground.

Embracing advancement is basic to the progress of any business. By making a culture of development, putting resources into new advancements, and empowering imagination and trial and error, organizations can remain on the ball and stay serious in their industry. It is vital to recall that development is a continuous cycle, and organizations should adjust and advance to remain ahead.

Systems for Business Nimbleness

Business dexterity alludes to flexibility, which can assist organizations with staying serious and effective when economic situations change. You can accomplish business spryness by carrying out compelling systems and making objectives that reference the organization mission for direction. Learning the various ways of further developing business nimbleness can assist you with fostering an itemized methodology for your association.

What is business dexterity?

Business dexterity is the capacity to adjust to changing business circumstances including markets, customers and creation. A spry business might have the option to flourish and accomplish an upper hand notwithstanding these progressions since it's ready to develop with the business and its clients. Business dexterity expects associations to further develop activities connecting with regions like innovation, funds and regulation. Associations can likewise further develop methodology, creation, promoting, security and client care.

For what reason is business deftness significant?

Business deftness is significant in light of the fact that this adaptability can keep an association functional when changes happen. Since the market in many ventures can change all of a sudden, it's vital to have the option to adjust and change your business system to stay fruitful in a variable climate. Business readiness is additionally significant in giving consumer loyalty. Shoppers are bound to be faithful to an organization on the off chance that its items reliably get to the next level.

Step by step instructions to gauge business dexterity

1. Characterize organization mission

The organization mission is an explanation that mirrors the association's guiding principle and a dream that you need to achieve. Having a mission is a significant piece of making a field-tested strategy since it decides how to decide and educates the improvement regarding functional systems.

You can characterize an organization mission by distinguishing what is critical to your association and picking a drawn out objective that you need to achieve through your organization. For instance, in the event that you are a tech organization, your organization mission might be to make imaginative items and make it simpler to store and access data with mechanical gadgets.

2. Make objectives

Involving your organization mission as an aide, you can make objectives that assist with accomplishing your vision. Your objectives additionally assist the association with becoming adaptable and adjust to changes in the business' current circumstance. While making an objective, guarantee that you can quantify its result. You can do this by making a cutoff time and recognizing pertinent measurements to follow all through the execution cycle. You can utilize measurements, for example, change rates, maintenance, income or consumer loyalty to quantify your objectives. Associations can utilize Brilliant objectives to make powerful plans.

3. Foster a system

A system is a progression of steps that guide you or a group toward achieving an objective. To foster a procedure, figure out which errands the group should finish to accomplish a specific result. Then, characterize each undertaking so a group can play out each move toward the system. Fostering a methodology likewise expects you to figure out which workers are a piece of achieving the objective, which can assist with designating errands. A procedure likewise gives a timetable and timetable to an undertaking and its errands.

4. Execute your procedure

The subsequent stage in having the option to gauge the spryness of your business is to carry out the methodology among your workers. Fruitful procedures can decidedly influence the workplace, representatives and the items the organization produces, which can prompt consumer loyalty. Carrying out a procedure requires pioneers who can give direction and backing to workers when they are encountering a change. It's essential to reinforce correspondence and guarantee that workers get direct guidelines so that they're ready to get done with their jobs.

5. Utilize key measurements to evaluate objectives

When you carry out and execute a methodology, you utilize the measurements you recently recognized to check its prosperity. Assuming you achieve the objective, you could involve these equivalent measurements while executing comparable systems later on. In the event that you don't achieve your objective, consider returning to how to best track the progressions you need to execute.

Step by step instructions to further develop business spryness

This are tips en route to further develop business readiness in your association:

Focus on the clients

Keeping an effective business depends on having clients and having the option to develop your client base. As well as offering some incentive to the client by means of advertising, creation and dispersion, streamlining client assistance can likewise assist with guaranteeing that the organization is focusing on the requirements of its clients. You can demand criticism from clients with studies to find out about their cravings and necessities. Expanding client commitment through virtual entertainment, email crusades and in-person collaborations can likewise decidedly affect consumer loyalty.

Put resources into new advancements

Mechanical headways are one of the essential drivers of business change and development.

Organizations might stay cutthroat by putting resources into these new advances and integrating innovation into their business activities. For instance, refreshing working frameworks can assist processes with turning out to be more effective, which can add to quicker creation and conveyance of the item to clients. Innovation can likewise assist with further developing client communications. For instance, online entertainment stages give a reasonable and effectively available technique to associate with shoppers.

Foster solid authority inside the organization

Gifted pioneers can assist with facilitating advances and advance inspiration when the organization is evolving. A compelling pioneer can acquaint advancement and foster ways with further develop both organization cycles and worker abilities. A few characteristics of talented pioneers incorporate viable correspondence and clearness of thoughts.

Reinforce the labor force

Organizations that need to be adaptable could focus on recruiting nimble workers. Improving employing processes assists find with peopling who can add to the organization mission and upgrade the organization culture. Giving broad preparation and expert advancement valuable open doors is likewise advantageous to representatives and can assist them with creating ranges of abilities to further develop business spryness.

The critical parts of business nimbleness include:

- **Culture**. Business deftness is established on areas of strength for a culture with practices, values, and perspectives that work with adaptability and flexibility. Such a culture permits an association to answer rapidly to changing circumstances during questionable times.

- **Administration**. Business deftness requires great administration of the inner cycles and designs to work with better navigation, straightforwardness, and responsibility.

- **Administration**. Lithe authority includes cooperative ways to deal with assistance associations get by in groundbreaking times. As opposed to settling on all choices alone, coordinated pioneers engage junior staff individuals by appointing various undertakings, making it simple to accomplish shared objectives.

- **Technique**. Associations comprehend the vital targets and conditions of their methodologies and make suitable adjustments to answer startling occasions in the business climate.

- **Individuals**. Workers are pivotal partners in any association. To accomplish business readiness, great supervisors work on their representatives' abilities to team up and answer well to changing economic situations.

A nimble business has the accompanying attributes:

- **Responsive**. Spry associations answer rapidly to changes in economic situations, permitting them to get by and flourish.
- **Creative**. As spry associations adjust to vulnerabilities, they track down better approaches for getting things done. They likewise make new items and administrations, which help become their endlessly piece of the pie.
- **Versatile**. Nimble associations utilize adaptable procedures to change and apply to new circumstances.
- **Level design**. Nimble associations have a level hierarchical design, imparting choices to other colleagues. A level construction empowers organizations to change their tasks rapidly during vulnerability.
- **Representative strengthening.** Light-footed associations enable representatives through clear assumptions,

task appointment, preparing and advancement, great remuneration, and prizes. Thus, workers have high assurance and the right abilities to assist the business with making due during attempting times.

- **Solid culture.** Establishments have a nimble culture that favors cooperation and joint effort, reasonableness, adaptability, trust, and great correspondence, empowering them to adjust effectively to showcase changes.

CHAPTER 9:

The Fate of Abundance: Manageability and Heritage

As the overall scene goes through massive changes in monetary issues, advancement, and social characteristics, the possibility of overflow is creating past basic financial flood. The possible destiny of overflow is becoming indivisible from sensibility, including financial prospering as well as environmental commitment, social impact, and the creation of overcoming legacies. This guide expects to edify the way toward a sweeping method for managing wealth, considering both the reasonability of resources and the continuing on through impact individuals and associations can leave for individuals later on.

Rethinking Overflow in the 21st 100 years

Past Money related Flood: Reevaluating overflow to integrate monetary assets as well as a greater scope of resources, including time, data, and social capital.

The Acceptable Overflow Perspective: Introducing the possibility of affordable wealth, where money related flourishing exists along with biological stewardship, social worth, and moral vital methodologies.

Moving Characteristics: Examining the changing potential gains of individuals and associations, underlining the journey for reason, meaning, and a beneficial outcome on the world.

The Intersection point of Wealth and Sensibility

Normal Commitment: Taking a gander at the particular employment of viable practices in overflow creation, from eco-obliging hypotheses to green business methodology.

Social Impact: Looking at the meaning of changing overflow creation to social commitment, including liberality, moral vital methodologies, and neighborhood.

Corporate Social Commitment (CSR): Analyzing how associations can integrate CSR crashes into their middle frameworks, adding to both financial accomplishment and positive social outcomes.

Viable Cash the board and Financial Planning

Regular, Social, and Organization (ESG) Powerful cash the executives: Exploring the rising of ESG estimates in hypothesis decisions, where biological, social, and organization factors are seen as nearby financial estimations.

Impact Viable cash the executives: Diving into impact powerful monetary preparation, where financial hypotheses are made with the unequivocal assumption for delivering quantifiable social or normal benefits.

Reasonable Money related Planning: Analyzing how individuals and associations can incorporate legitimacy into their financial arrangement, changing theories to individual characteristics and long stretch practicality goals.

Development and the Difference in Overflow The board

Fintech Courses of action: Analyzing the impact of money related development (fintech) on overflow the chiefs, including robo-guides, online stages, and blockchain applications.

High level Financial principles and the Destiny of Trades: Examining the occupation of mechanized money related structures, including computerized monetary standards, in reshaping how overflow is executed and taken care of.

Data Assessment in Overflow The leaders: Discussing the usage of data examination in propelling hypothesis decisions, risk the board, and redid money related readiness.

Building and Saving Legacies

Legacy Orchestrating: Researching methods for building and safeguarding legacies, including home planning, movement making courses of action for associations, and the trading of values across ages.

Enlightening Legacy: Looking at the meaning of tutoring as a legacy, recalling hypotheses for data, skill improvement, and the reinforcing of individuals later on.

Social and Inventive Legacy: Inspecting how individuals and associations can add to social and innovative legacies, saving and progressing creative articulations for the headway of society.

Investigating Troubles and Risks in Overflow The board

Climate Related Risks: Looking at the impact of ecological change on overflow protection and techniques for regulating climate related bets in hypotheses.

Moral Hardships: Keeping an eye on moral challenges in overflow the chiefs, incorporating issues associated with straightforwardness, fair essential strategies, and reliable organization.

Between generational Overflow Move: Taking a gander at the complexities of getting overflow across ages, including the potential for conflicts, charge ideas, and the meaning of open correspondence.

Liberality and Social Undertaking

Key Benevolence: Discussing the possibility of crucial unselfishness, where selfless surrendering is fixed with greater goals and social impact.

Social Undertaking: Exploring the combination of business and social impact, highlighting how social business visionaries impact business principles for positive change.

Total Impact: Analyzing the capacity of agreeable undertakings, where individuals, associations, and affiliations get together for total impact on cordial and environmental issues.

Future Examples and Anticipated Developments

The Rising of Insightful Commercialization: Researching how purchaser tendencies are driving associations to embrace sensible practices and add to social and normal causes.

Regulatory Changes: Separating the propelling scene of rules and approaches that engage sensible key arrangements and fit overflow the chiefs.

The Occupation of Preparing: Looking at the meaning of tutoring in shaping the possible destiny of overflow, empowering individuals with the data and capacities to seek after taught and moral financial decisions.

Embracing Some other Season of Overflow

The possible destiny of overflow is going through a pivotal development, embracing reasonability, social impact, and the arrangement of getting through legacies. As individuals and associations investigate this creating scene, they are called to reevaluate standard contemplations of progress and embrace a thorough method for managing overflow creation. By coordinating legitimacy into money related readiness, placing assets into huge drives, and leaving persisting through legacies, individuals and associations can add to a future where overflow isn't simply assessed in financial terms yet furthermore in the positive and getting through changes made to serve society and the planet.

Making an Enduring Effect

Having an enduring effect on your clients is fundamental for building fruitful, long haul connections.

It doesn't make any difference on the off chance that you're an entrepreneur or a carefully prepared President, carrying out strong techniques can have a significant effect.

One of the vital parts of having an enduring effect is understanding and talking your image voice.

It is essential to impart in a manner that reverberates with your crowd and addresses your image genuinely.

You can do this by talking in your image's voice and conveying it in your discussions with clients, permitting you to make major areas of strength for a that will have an enduring effect.

The following are 5 strong systems that will assist you with having an enduring effect on your clients and take your business to a higher level.

1. Building solid associations with your clients is urgent for the progress of your business: When you have an enduring effect, you make steadfast clients who are bound to allude you to other people and keep working with you over the long haul.

By reliably surpassing their assumptions, you will end up being their go-to answer for their necessities.

To have an enduring effect, you really want to zero in on understanding and addressing your clients' necessities and objectives. This requires going underneath the level and really getting to know their qualities and their short-and long haul objectives.

At the point when you exhibit that you figure out their remarkable difficulties and can give custom-made arrangements, you lay out trust and validity.

2. To have an enduring effect on your clients, you should grasp their necessities and objectives: This requires undivided attention and successful correspondence: Pose unassuming inquiries and Pay attention to their reactions. This will assist you with acquiring important experiences into their inspirations and needs.

When you have an unmistakable comprehension of their requirements and objectives, you can adjust your items or administrations to address those issues.

At the point when you show them that you are put resources into their prosperity, you secure yourself as a significant accomplice instead of simply one more specialist co-op. You become a "confided in source".

3. Viable correspondence is the groundwork of any fruitful client relationship: Laying out clear and open lines of correspondence all along is fundamental.

This should be possible by consistently registering to guarantee their fulfillment and tending to any worries or input they could have.

While speaking with your clients, communicating in their language is significant.

This implies utilizing wording and tone that impacts them, zeroing in on making yourself clear in a way that is straightforward and is engaging to their objectives.

On the off chance that you have not taken in the particulars of an extraordinary device - Circle Evaluations, you should call me about it. Information on this device has been demonstrated to further develop correspondence, which prompts better client care. A short preparation will bring you prompt comprehension and knowledge!

4. Remarkable client support is vital to having an enduring effect on your clients: When your clients feel esteemed and upheld, they are bound to stay faithful and prescribe your business to other people.

Do an amazing job to surpass their assumptions. Expect their necessities and proactively offer arrangements or assets that can assist them with accomplishing their objectives.

Give clear and definite data about your items or administrations and be receptive to their inquiries.

5. Personalization is an integral asset for having an enduring effect on your clients: Designer your collaborations to your clients' remarkable inclinations and necessities.

At the point when you show your clients that you comprehend their singular necessities and inclinations, you make a feeling of selectiveness and fortify your relationship.

Having an enduring effect on your clients isn't just about quick achievement; it's tied in with building a long haul, commonly useful relationship.

At the point when you put resources into figuring out your clients' necessities, giving uncommon client care, and customizing their encounters, you make major areas of strength for a for enduring achievement.

Keep in mind, having an enduring effect takes devotion, validness, and a real obligation to your clients' prosperity.

Passing on Your Business Inheritance

What does the following period of your business have coming up? Assemble your privately-run company so your inheritance lives on for your replacements.

For some business visionaries, developing a fruitful private venture from the beginning the encapsulation of the Pursuit of happiness. What's more, whether you began your organization to help your family or as an individual undertaking, you might maintain that it should outlive you. You put a great deal of work in and your representatives and clients won't maintain that your entryways should close. Anyway, how would you deal with your business inheritance?

In the event that you're quick to fire up your own private company to make a heritage for people in the future, this is the very thing you really want to be aware!

Plan for the Future all along

Business visionary places that one key to building your own business heritage is to "begin considering the end." By zeroing in on your ultimate objective for your business heritage, you'll have the option to set out an unmistakable arrangement to arrive. Do you maintain that your family should acquire the business? Do you believe that they should work for the business? Assuming this is the case, will they get priority over additional certified competitors? How might your business structure affect progression - will your replacement be getting shares in an enterprise or assuming control over a sole ownership?

You don't be guaranteed to need to address these inquiries immediately as you fire up your business, yet you ought to have them at the top of the priority list. When your business is more settled, you can begin work on a conventional progression plan.

Making A Progression Plan

At the point when you work with your merchants and clients, you utilize formal agreements. Your business progression plan ought to be the same - it will altogether affect how things play out once you pass the business on. You would rather not leave without an arrangement set up; that can leave an enormous (and costly) legitimate wreck that your replacements and workers should figure out. It implies the business will not really be run by your vision or that your replacements may not get what you planned. It can cause a ton of hardship in your loved ones. It might try and mean the business can't proceed.

At the end of the day, a formal, legitimately restricting progression plan is a flat out need. Meet with your lawyer and business guides to examine and draft an unmistakable business progression plan. Begin the progression arranging process early (for example before you're confronting a difficult disease or other issue) so you can deal with it with an unmistakable head.

An intensive progression plan ought to address both what happens when the pioneer ventures down. It ought to likewise address what happens when there are numerous proprietors and somebody needs out.

Issues to consider include:

- Who will maintain the business after you (or how a replacement will be picked)

- How responsibility for business will be given to your replacements

- What the assessment suggestions are and the way that you need to manage them

- The interaction for purchasing out a proprietor that no longer needs to be involved (which might burden the income)

- Expectations with respect to possession (for example does proprietorship need to give to relatives or can non-relatives acquire?)

Progression arranging is more muddled the greater and complex your business is. Yet, even little, straightforward organizations need an unmistakable arrangement on the off chance that you believe the business should make due for different ages.

Get some margin to meet with a lawyer to sort through a progression plan. They can assist you with setting up the essential legitimate and monetary designs to ensure the interaction chugs along as expected (and as indicated by your desires).

What's more, recall that your progression plan isn't firmly established. As your business develops and your conditions change, you'll have to refresh your arrangement to ensure every one of the applicable issues are covered.

Set Up Your Variety of things to take care of All alone

One of the main pieces of your progression plan is the means by which your replacement will be picked. At times, your kids might need to step in and run the organization. Your progression plan ought to cover that - whether family will get priority over different up-and-comers, for instance, or what occurs if a youngster needs to work for the organization and there's no vacant position.

Yet, your children or replacements will not be guaranteed to share your enthusiasm for your work. They might have their own arrangements for their vocations. You'll have to anticipate that, as well. Ensure there are arrangements for recruiting a non-relative to run the organization once you step down - you don't maintain that the business should go to pieces in light of the fact that your kids would rather not be straightforwardly involved. They're still proprietors will in any case profit from the business proceeding to work.

As a component of your arrangement for a non-relative coming in to maintain the business, you'll need to address keeping your replacements engaged with the business. Contingent upon the size and nature of your business, that might mean conveying normal updates or having standard gatherings. Furthermore, recall - investors need to decide on significant issues. They eventually control the organization. So in the event that you're coordinated as a company, try to converse with your lawyer about how your replacements will included proceed.

Illuminate Your Replacements Early

Your replacements need to know how the business will be passed along. You would rather not pass on them out of the loop and power them to manage everything as a shock. For your business to endure when you step down, your replacements should be prepared to deal with it.

It's smart to teach your youngsters on some business rudiments. That implies perusing budget reports, understanding your business design, and knowing how to practice their privileges as proprietors. Keep them required all along so they're OK with your business and with their part in its future.

You ought to likewise converse with your replacements about how they see themselves being associated with the business later on. You might find that they care very little about working for the business, and that is not a problem! They could have their own vocation objectives, very much as you did when you began the business. They might not have a talent for what you do or might need to achieve something all alone without your assistance. In the event that they take over in light of the fact that they feel committed, they'll be despondent - and they may not be the most ideal decision to run the organization.

Impart plainly about your vision and ensure your family comprehends what's happening -

straightforwardness is the smartest idea to safeguard your business inheritance.

As well as telling your replacements going to happen when you pass the rod, you ought to ensure they knew about your workers and supervisory crew. You don't maintain that the proprietors and the administration should be outsiders - they will should agreeable work together. Also, assuming your replacements intend to work for the organization, your representatives will need to be know all about them. Your representatives might be stressed over nepotism - that your replacements might wind up in administration without capabilities. Ensuring your main beneficiaries, the board, and workers are know all about one another can assist with facilitating those issues.

Look Past Your Genealogical record

It might appear to be outlandish to hear that one of the ways of making your inheritance business a triumph is to employ beyond your loved ones.

Having areas of strength for a group and expert worker support is pivotal to proceeding with the progress of your inheritance business throughout the long term. As we referenced above, you must have arrangements in your progression plan for employing outside administration. It may not actually be an issue of your main beneficiaries not having any desire to run the organization - they may simply be excessively youthful!

An expert supervisory group will have the experience important to help your business through the change away from your initiative and keep things running. They'll likewise have the option to take a gander at your activity with a new perspective and assist with making certain about what makes your business a triumph and what might be smarter to change.

What's more, outside administration or no, you ought to truly think about setting up an external Directorate on the off chance that you're coordinated as an enterprise. Search for a gathering with experience in your industry and related businesses. They can assist with directing the organization and safeguard the interests of the proprietors, regardless of who's maintaining the business.

At last, remember to converse with your workers. They realize that you won't be running the organization always and they will have questions. They'll want to find out whether the business will continue to work after you resign or die. They'll need to realize that you have an arrangement for when that occurs. They might have worries about your kids or main beneficiaries stepping in without the right capabilities. You don't need to share the particulars as a whole, obviously, however you ought to tell them what the progression plan by and large resembles and ensure they realize they can carry their interests to you.

Allow Your Business To live On

As a business person, you're as of now forward-looking. You put a ton of work and energy into your business and you need it to endure into what's to come. In a perfect world, you believe it should go past your kids or beneficiaries and on to people in the future - perhaps in ceaselessness! However, that sort of business life expectancy doesn't simply occur. It takes cautious preparation front and center to ensure that your replacements and the business are safeguarded. You want a reasonable interaction for the progress and you really want to ensure your workers and replacements figure out it. Then, at that point, you can resign with the genuine serenity that your business will live on to help your replacements and people in the future.

Conclusion

Determination: A Guide to Business Abundance Without Second thoughts

As we explore the consistently changing scene of overflow creation, flourishing has progressed past straightforward financial conglomeration. It has woven itself into the surface of practicality, social impact, and the helping through legacy we leave. This trip, typified as "A Manual for Business Overflow Without Doubts," invites us to envision result in monetary terms as well as to leave on an exhaustive pursuit where each step is purposeful, deliberate, and missing any hint of disappointment.

In this aide, legitimacy goes probably as the compass, guiding us towards hypotheses that resonation commitment to our ongoing situation and society. The segments spread out with methods that transcend standard wealth, embracing the ethos of regular stewardship, moral vital strategies, and a guarantee to impacting the world forever.

Development, the driver of historic change, pushes us ahead, reshaping overflow the board with fintech plans, high level money related principles, and the logical capacity of data. These mechanical types of progress smooth out our money related methodology as well as empower us to make taught, future-focused decisions.

In any case, our cycle loosens up past the constraints of the financial space. It incorporates the delicate specialty of legacy building, where we make accounts of course and pass on overflow as well as cleverness, data, and a critical social and inventive inheritance. It prompts us to contemplate the between generational trade of values, with each age staying on the shoulders of the one going before, propped by the understanding procured from triumphs and troubles something similar.

Despite risks and hardships, we remain steadfast. Climate related weaknesses, moral ties, and the intricacies of between generational overflow move are not street blocks but rather likely opportunities to show adaptability and a guarantee to principled free heading.

Good cause and social undertaking emerge as fundamental areas, calling us to take part in fundamental giving, weaving our business sharpness eagerly for positive change. Total impact transforms into the mantra, featuring the force of helpful undertakings in keeping an eye on social and environmental concerns.

As we wrap up this phenomenal trip, envision your business as an overflow generator as well as an influence for good — a reference point of reasonability, a stimulus for positive change, and a legacy that transcends cash related measures. Embrace this manual for business overflow without regrets, where every decision is a phase towards a future where thriving isn't simply procured at this point shared, and accomplishment is assessed by money related benefit as well as by the persisting through impact on ages to come.

In this end part, I stand at the union of custom and headway, drawing from the knowledge of the past to edify the far ahead. Let this guide your business takes a stab at, controlling you towards a future where overflow isn't just assembled at this point shared, assessed in numbers as well as in the beneficial outcomes had on the world — a trip to business overflow without mourns, where every decision rehashes the commitment to a prosperous and conservative future.

www.ingramcontent.com/pod-product-compliance
Lightning Source LLC
Chambersburg PA
CBHW071029290526
45795CB00004B/1152

* 9 7 9 8 8 8 0 1 0 9 2 7 2 *